THE
SURVIVAL HOT LIST

THE
SURVIVAL HOT LIST

Conquering the Seven Deadly Trends

SECOND EDITION

Joseph A. Bagnall

iUniverse, Inc.
New York   Bloomington

THE SURVIVAL HOT LIST
Conquering the Seven Deadly Trends

Copyright © 2010 Joseph Bagnall

iUniverse books may be ordered through booksellers or by contacting:

iUniverse
1663 Liberty Drive
Bloomington, IN 47403
www.iuniverse.com
1-800-Authors (1-800-288-4677)

Because of the dynamic nature of the Internet, any Web addresses or links contained in this book may have changed since publication and may no longer be valid. The views expressed in this work are solely those of the author and do not necessarily reflect the views of the publisher, and the publisher hereby disclaims any responsibility for them.

ISBN: 978-0-595-37958-3 (pbk)
ISBN: 978-0-595-82327-7 (ebk)

Printed in the United States of America

iUniverse rev. date: 6/15/2010

Photo Credits

President Franklin D. Roosevelt Franklin D. Roosevelt Presidential Library and Museum

Albert Einstein Library of Congress Prints and Photographs Division Digital ID eph.3b46036

Edward Teller Lawrence Livermore National Laboratory Photo

President Harry S. Truman U.S. Army Film Courtesy of the Harry S. Truman Library

President Dwight D. Eisenhower Courtesy of the Dwight D. Eisenhower Library

Chief Justice Earl Warren Harris and Ewing photography firm whose works have all lapsed into the public domain.

Norman Cousins PD-USGOV-NASA

Walter Cronkite Steve Friedman Copyright 1996, CBS Inc. All rights reserved. (#86005) Used with permission.

President George H. W. Bush Official White House Photo Library of Congress Prints and Photographs Division.

President John F. Kennedy Portrait distributed by the White House. Image courtesy of the John F. Kennedy Presidential Library and Museum

John F. Kennedy John F. Kennedy Presidential Library and Museum Photo No. Kn24677

President Woodrow Wilson Library of Congress Prints and Photographs Division

Eleanor Roosevelt Franklin D. Roosevelt Presidential Library and Museum

President Jimmy Carter Official White House Photograph Library of Congress No. 31JA77 0324

To

The American Federal Union
Past, Present, and Future

"My Dream is of a place and time where America will once again
be seen as the last best hope on earth"––Abraham Lincoln

Acknowledgments

I am deeply grateful to my wife, Naomi, and my daughter, Ashley, for assistance in preparing the manuscript.

Prologue

"The dogmas of the quiet past are inadequate to the stormy present. The occasion is piled high with difficulty, and we must rise with the occasion. As our case is new, so we must think anew and act anew. We must disenthrall ourselves."

–Abraham Lincoln

"Now the Trumpet summons us again—not as a call to bear arms, though arms we need—but a call to bear the burden of a long twilight struggle, year in and year out, rejoicing in hope, patient in tribulation—a struggle against the common enemies of man: tyranny, poverty, disease and war itself. Can we forge against these enemies A Grand and Global Alliance, north and south, east and west, that can assure a more fruitful life for all mankind? Will you join in that historic effort?"

–John F. Kennedy

"The only limit to our realization of tomorrow will be our doubts of today. Let us move forward with strong and active faith."

–Franklin D. Roosevelt

Contents

Introduction

In a panel discussion at Boston College in late autumn of 2004, the distinguished political scientist, James MacGregor Burns, lamented that 45 to 50 percent of potential American voters fail to show up at the polls. When these non-voters are asked why they do not vote, he said, the answer most commonly given was that it didn't matter. Voting makes no difference.

The issues presented in *The Survival Hot List: Conquering the Seven Deadly Trends,* will make a difference. Chances are slim that civilization as we know it will survive in the 21ˢᵗ Century, if the Seven Deadly Trends are not resolved internationally, in timely fashion. The Seven Deadly Trends are: 1) The Thermonuclear Threat to all Life on Earth, 2) Destruction of Rain Forests, 3) Global Warming, 4) Ozone Depletion, 5) Acid Rain, 6) Population Explosion and 7) All Forms of Military Aggression.

The format of *this book* draws upon a Socratic framework, teaching by posing fifteen vital questions that proceed through three brief chapters. The fifteen questions deal with substantive survival issues–not the kind that are entertainingly resolved in the Darwinian games presented on popular television shows– but real, life-threatening, thermonuclear and environmental issues. These issues were once given high priority, but they are now lost in a massive stream of "information age" trivia and the shallow tides of political conservatism.

It will no doubt seem odd that the author posses questions to himself and then answers them. Traditional Socratic teaching involves posing questions to students who are asked to respond. But in this case students have not been given much information on the subject at hand. They are aware, for the most part, of a few contemporary tinkerers who are attempting to address enormous survival issues. But without a modification of the Socratic format, it would be impossible to present a pantheon of statesmen and a plethora of new material for their consideration.

The author's answers to the fifteen questions derive from the thought and teachings of great American statesmen, scientists, historians and philosophers. Fifteen of them are specifically cited in matters concerning the development of world law. My own contribution includes the proposal to develop a world federal system patterned after the American federal system and the attendant Resolution of Interdependence.

This book is a polemic which is presented without apology. It contains the priority questions for our time, questions that could be posed and discussed freely a generation ago, but are now ridiculed and dismissed by the ignorant, the timid, and the corrupt. Arguments against collective security and the United Nations are found everywhere. They overwhelm us in a manner that begs for a strong polemic, a counter argument without compromise or equivocation.

This is my final summary of important things. It is a record of my own view that the significance of American history is that it provides a cognitive road map to a viable, safe world. This is my life statement. I am also presenting the survival perspectives of the finest leaders in my lifetime. The wisdom of the past is here on display.

The appendices of this book contain documents that are not found in other books. The American public knows little or nothing about the Universal Declaration of Human Rights, or The Charter of the United Nations and the Statute of the International Court of Justice. These are offered as points of reference in a serious work for serious times.

Joseph A. Bagnall
Oceanside, California
May 2010

CHAPTER ONE
Identifying Survival Issues

I. WHAT ARE THE SPECIFIC SURVIVAL ISSUES OF OUR TIME?

Survival in early 21st Century America is a widespread and enormous concern. We are all preoccupied with the day-to-day challenges of making a living. We struggle to survive in a competitive America dedicated to the ideals of economic gain and material comfort. We read books about habits of effective people and strategies for successful competition. We snuggle into comfortable places and indulge our critical need for escapism, watching juvenile Darwinian elimination games on television. We honor the force and cunning of those who win; and we glorify the predators who hog the most loot, but we pay virtually no attention to serious discussion about **surviving** the ominous thermonuclear and environmental threats that are dogging our footsteps.

Most of us have not found the time, the wisdom, or the courage to think seriously about a more comprehensive survival perspective. Nor have we been prepared, by academia or by the media, to confront the **major survival issues** of our time.

Calling for our immediate attention is *The Survival Hot List*; namely, The

Thermonuclear Threat to all Life on Earth, Destruction of Rain Forests, Global Warming, Ozone Depletion, Acid Rain, Population Explosion, and all forms of Military Aggression. Can we conquer these *Seven Deadly Trends?*

1. The Thermonuclear Threat to all Life on Earth

Nuclear proliferation is an important facet of this deadly trend, but there is a simultaneous spread of chemical, biological and radiological weapons as well. Even so, since nuclear stockpiles worldwide would seem to exceed the quantity of other weapons of mass destruction, the problem of control of nuclear weapons will be given priority in this account.

We have been reminded that thermonuclear attack could occur in America. Nuclear weapons could be smuggled in by terrorists or delivered from the air, we are told. But those who remind us are tinkerers who have demonstrated little knowledge of the problem and are rapidly destroying vital international programs that have been painfully crafted by the statesmen of the past.

On August 6, 1945, a thirteen kiloton atomic bomb was dropped on Hiroshima, Japan. In a matter of moments 129, 558 persons were killed or injured. Three days later a twenty-two kiloton atomic bomb was dropped on Nagasaki, Japan with similar ghastly results.

With the advent of the H-Bomb in the 1950s, the atomic bomb had a new, minor function. It was only the trigger on the H-Bomb. While fearsome atomic weapons had previously been measured in the kiloton range–a twenty kiloton bomb was the equivalent of twenty thousand tons of TNT– the new hydrogen bombs had explosive capacity in the megaton range; that is, a twenty megaton bomb was the equivalent of twenty million tons of TNT.

If only one fifteen megaton hydrogen bomb were to be detonated, with an atomic trigger, fifteen miles above a target, the resultant damage would include a crater about 440 feet deep with a five mile circumference. It would also throw out firestorms for fifty miles in each direction, and the center of the blast would be the temperature of the sun.

This hellish scenario would result from only one bomb, deliverable by one missile. In the event of an attack with many bombs, there is no conceivable evacuation plan or technological fix that would keep America safe.

President John F. Kennedy gave us the best survival perspective when he spoke before the United Nations General Assembly on September 25, 1961. He pled for a *world security system* and then issued this dire warning, "... together we shall save our planet, or together we shall perish in its flames. Save it we can—and save it we must—and then shall we earn the eternal thanks of mankind, and as peacemakers, the eternal blessings of God."

2. Destruction of Rain Forests

The rain forests of planet earth are being destroyed to sell timber, to provide for banana plantations or cattle ranches, or among other things, to provide charcoal for industrial plants.

Since 1945, over 40% of rain forests worldwide have been destroyed. They are gone forever. As we continue to destroy the rain forests, over fifty species of plants and animals are permanently eliminated each day. Since one in four medicines contains compounds that were originally obtained from rain forest species, the opportunities to discover new medicines are rapidly disappearing.

Tropical rain forests are vital to the world's weather patterns. When the rain forest canopy is removed, the sun's radiation is bounced back from the barren remains. This so-called albedo effect results in alteration of wind currents, a violent interruption of convection currents, an increased rainfall in some areas of the world, and decreased rainfall in others. The destruction of rain forests also affects the balance of carbon dioxide in the atmosphere. Rain forests have been called the lungs of the world.

3. Global Warming

Global warming is associated with a global greenhouse canopy created by man-made methane, carbon dioxide, and other gases which have appeared in ever greater quantities since the onset of the industrial revolution.

It has taken nature about 10,000 years for global temperatures to raise 5 degrees Celsius. Many scientists predict that a comparable rise of 5 degrees will take place sometime between the next seventy-five to one hundred years. This swift change could result in diminished water supplies in populated areas, significant melting of ice caps, flooding of existing shorelines, and alteration of the map of the world, the conversion of productive agricultural lands to deserts, increased air pollution, floods and hurricanes, and the expansion of tropical diseases worldwide.

Our Environmental Protection Agency has noted that most of these trends are significantly underway. To ignore them will lead to catastrophic disruptions to the life we know.

4. Ozone depletion

In the year 2000, the Environmental Protection Agency confirmed that the ozone hole over the Antarctic covered an area larger than the North American continent. In September 2006, NASA confirmed that the average area of the ozone hole was the largest ever observed. The resultant increase in UV-B rays bombards all living things. In practical human terms this means an increase in skin cancer and cataract cases worldwide. UV-B will also weaken human and animal immune systems and impair photosynthesis and plant metabolism. And finally UV-B rays will penetrate the oceans, causing a slower growth rate of plankton, thereby reducing available sea life.

5. Acid Rain

Acid rain occurs when sulfur dioxide and nitrogen oxides are released into our atmosphere from the use of coal, from base metal smelting, and from fuel combustion in automobiles.

In some areas of Canada the rain has been highly acidic. As a result, a large part of the Salmon habitat in the Maritimes has been lost, and Eastern Canada's forests are in rapid decline. The Red Spruce are dying in Vermont, New Hampshire, and North Carolina, while the Black Forest in Germany, and the forests of Eastern Europe are being obliterated by acid rain as well.

Damage to buildings and monuments has been documented in Canada and Europe, and ancient stonework and statuary is being corroded, fractured, and discolored in various parts of the world.

And what is acid rain doing to aquatic ecosystems? Acid rain causes harmful mosses and plankton that invades lakes– with an attendant loss of fish. Canada has over 18,000 dying lakes. In recent times, two thousand had no fish at all.

The restoration of acid lakes is currently underway in Europe, Northeastern United States and Canada. The restoration process sometimes involves the adding of calcium carbonate. This so-called liming must continue as long as we produce acid rain

6. Population Explosion

Thomas Robert Malthus (1776-1834) advanced the theory that population tends to increase at a faster rate than its means of subsistence and that widespread poverty and degradation are the result, unless population is preventively limited through moral restraint, or limited though disease, famine, or war.

Arguments against this Malthusian theory have been advanced from the political left to the right and every point on the political spectrum in between. In spite of this, it seems reasonable to assert that the projected increase in human population worldwide is bound to create poverty and disease and will exacerbate all of the nuclear and environmental crises. It also seems reasonable to assert that excessive population might be limited preventively, through a system of international incentives for separate nations.

7. All Forms of Military Aggression

Terrorism is a form of military aggression. It is also a worldwide phenomenon that calls for a worldwide solution. Unilateral preemptive responses to perceived terror are a disastrous U.S. policy. In effect we are engaging in the same tactic that we have traditionally condemned. Also, if other nations choose the same foolish approach, the result will be a complete breakdown of international order.

Unilateral Preemptive First Strike is a radical departure from the traditional American approach in foreign affairs. Since the dawn of the atomic age, the U.S. has led in the effort to promote collective security, to contain adversarial threats, and to employ measured and judicious collective responses to curb aggression. For half a century we have condemned and opposed aggression and held the moral high ground. These policies have led to a successful collective defense of the Republic of Korea against North Korean aggression and a masterful curb on Iraqi aggression against Kuwait. In this latter so-called Desert Storm operation, George H. W. Bush organized the whole world in a successful effort to stop Iraq. Communists and capitalists, Jews and Arabs joined hands to curb aggression. But right wing ideologues immediately castigated the effort, and ridiculed the United Nations involvement.

George W. Bush surrounded himself with right wing ideologues who stopped the sanctions, removed the United Nations forces and conducted preemptive war against Iraq. This war has resulted in financial burdens that were not experienced in Desert Storm. The senior Bush and his advisors knew that collective security meant shared risks and shared costs. They also seemed to understand that when the U.S. fought in Vietnam, without allies, without a clear mission statement or exit strategy, we experienced a humiliating defeat.

Our involvement in Iraq was virtually without allies, without a credible, consistent, mission statement, and, before the Obama administration, without an exit strategy.

The religious right is strongly supporting aggression and force. Many of them believe that it is important to confront evil at all costs, and some of them are praying for Armageddon when God destroys all of the wicked and lifts those up whom he will save. The mushroom cloud therefore becomes an inevitability, and perhaps a welcomed event.

Unilateral preemptive war has damaged the NATO Alliance and the multilateral agreement known as the United Nations. It is incredible that the American people supported a preemptive first strike policy in 2005. Particularly when U.N. forces had Saddam Hussein contained and sanctions in place.

Consider the radical departure we have made from our proud past:

A) In World War I we fought for the dual purpose of making the world safe for democracy and bringing an end to all wars. President Wilson's **League of Nations was conceived to resolve problems without recourse to war.**

B) The Kellogg-Briand Pact was an achievement of the conservative Calvin Coolidge administration. Secretary of State Frank Kellogg teamed with the French foreign minister in 1928, to rally 62 nations as signatories to **an agreement that no nation would ever use war as an instrument of foreign policy. Secretary Kellogg won the Nobel Peace Prize,** and leaders of aggressor nations were prosecuted and executed after World War II at Nuremberg, utilizing the pledges made in the Kellogg-Briand Pact as part of the case against war crimes.

C) President Franklin Delano Roosevelt asked the Congress for a declaration of war in 1941 because of the "dastardly and unprovoked attack" by Japan. And after the war **the United Nations was created through American leadership and planted on American soil for the express purpose of** *halting aggression.*

D) President Harry S. Truman organized a United Nations Police force **for the purpose of containing North Korean aggression.**

E) The NATO military alliance was formed in 1949 **as a free world defense shield**. The alliance was designed to *contain aggression*, and the defining phrase in the treaty stated "an attack against one is an attack against all." The SEATO alliance of Southeast Asia was designed to *contain communist expansion* and aggression as well.

F) President Lyndon B. Johnson's mission in Vietnam was perhaps an attempt at containment, but it was *unilateral and without a clear mission statement*–aside from the assertion that we were there to prevent a communist takeover. If that was the mission, we failed.

G) President Jimmy Carter led a boycott of the Moscow Olympics and took other measures against the Soviet Union as **a protest against Soviet aggression in Afghanistan.**

H) President George Herbert Walker Bush earned the respect and support of the whole world when he organized capitalists and communists, Jews and Arabs, and other seemingly dissident elements into a collective security arrangement dubbed Desert Storm. The whole world participated under the authority of **unanimous U.N. Security Council Resolutions designed to curb Iraqi aggression against Kuwait.** This mission was accomplished swiftly and at minimal cost. President Bush spoke eloquently of his collective approach to aggression in an address delivered at Maxwell Air Force Base, Montgomery, Alabama on April 13, 1991. The title of his address was *"The Possibility of a New World Order: Unlocking the Promise of Freedom."*

But radical and dangerous as the George W. Bush preemptive first strike policy may be, it is only one of the seven deadly trends. All seven are moving inexorably forward, creating a battered and very tentative planet. The Doomsday Clock is ticking, ever closer to midnight. **The seven trends will not be resolved without a vigorous international response to them.** If we continue to ignore them, we will assuredly drift toward a grim, unintended fate. If we plan to meet thermonuclear and environmental challenges with crisis-to-crisis improvisation, we will also fail. But with the adoption of long range global policies involving all nations as active participants, we may survive. Our chances will be improved if we can create a full-fledged world security system. But our recent lack of focus on collective security and worldwide cooperation may have already destroyed the prospect for American survival in the 21st Century

II. What Are We Focusing on Today?

In the second Bush administration, the politically immature received a daily dose of political pabulum. Conservative politicians and the media spoon fed the masses with a barrage of gross distortions and distractions. Among these are the threat of gay marriage, the liberal plan to take away guns, the liberal crusade against Christmas and the Boy Scouts, the liberal assault on the Ten Commandments, and liberal disloyalty to our country and our troops.

These wedge issues are part of the "values crusade" of the conservative right wing. Neo-con political commentators and writers constantly use them as they rev up their puerile base with charges of "evil" and "treason."

Historical Roots of the Loyalty Issue

Right wing political paranoia has deep historical roots. When the Democratic party made Senator John Kerry the nominee in 2004, it was widely understood that he would be the candidate best prepared to withstand the coming Republican onslaught against Democrats whom they would brand unpatriotic if not traitors. It was difficult to smear John Kerry as a traitor, but they successfully convinced many voters that his service in Vietnam was brief and without merit, his three purple hearts were mere bruises, and his subsequent campaign against the Vietnam War was at the very least, unpatriotic.

Republicans then rallied around Bush and Cheney with support for extension of an unmodified Patriot Act. They didn't seem concerned that civil liberties would be quashed as a consequence. Many Democrats said that a police state was rapidly evolving. They refused to join those who touted the Bush-Cheney team as the resolute, dedicated protectors of the nation in a period of heightened terrorist threat. Some few Republican extremists clustered around the Ann Coulter fringe, hurling charges of treason at Democrats who had engaged in nothing more than loyal dissent.

How could Democrats know, well in advance, that Republicans would challenge the patriotism of their party, and of their candidate? The answer, of course, is that patriotism has been the battle cry of conservatives in American politics from the earliest days of the Republic.

When Thomas Jefferson ran for the Presidency at the turn of the 19th Century, he stood in bold relief as the revolutionary who had penned the Declaration of Independence. He was a genuine patriot who was smeared by conservative Federalists as an advocate of the dangerous ideas of the French Revolution. He was dubbed a "filthy Jacobin by conservatives who favored the rich and well born at home, and monarchial England, abroad. They not only conjured up images of French mobs and the guillotine, but they also attempted to destroy Jefferson with the same tactics employed by McCarthy-led extremists of mid 20th Century who used the cry "filthy Communist" to cast aspersions on American reformers and liberals.

To stop the Jeffersonian tide, conservative Federalists passed three reactionary laws: the first was called the Alien Act, and it gave President John Adams the power to deport dangerous aliens. Often there was little distinction made between Jeffersonian democrats and dangerous aliens. The second was called the Sedition Act. It made criticism of President Adams a crime. As a result Jeffersonian editors were arrested for exercising their right to free speech. And the third extended the period for attainment of citizenship from four to fourteen years. Since virtually all of the new immigrants supported Jefferson, this extension of the wait period to vote was the desperate capstone on legislation designed to cast Jeffersonian democrats as irresponsible rabble and dangerous traitors.

The elitist elements of the former Federalist Party formed a new Whig party in the Jacksonian era. They viewed Jacksonian Democracy as a plague. But by 1849, an even more extreme conservative faction in embarrassed the Whigs when they formed a secret society called The Order of the Star Spangled Banner. These counterfeit conservatives spawned a movement that rapidly became national. To preserve their cowardly secrecy, they responded to every question, "I know nothing about it." As a result, they were popularly labeled, "Know Nothings."

This Order of the Star Spangled Banner created the American Party, a self styled patriotic party, and in 1856, former President, Millard Fillmore was chosen as the party candidate. Its anti- immigrant, anti-Catholic, and pro-slavery venom doomed it to disgrace and defeat.

The Whigs were always quite apart from this extreme conservative fringe. They spawned great American leaders such as Henry Clay, Daniel Webster, and young Abraham Lincoln. None of these statesmen were tainted with the nonsense of the extreme right wing of their day.

The Hamiltonian heirs of the Whig tradition became the Republican Party we know today. Their first great leader, Abraham Lincoln, is widely held in the highest esteem. But for all of the solid achievements of early Republicans, the party was in serious error to "wave the bloody shirt" in election after election for the next forty years. Reviving Civil War memories with taunts of "Democrat traitors," they reminded voters of Republican virtue, the treasonous secession of the Democratic South; and with numerous parades, they showcased the splendor of the Grand Army of the Republic.

Modern Republicans kept the loyalty theme alive in the Truman administration. They captured both the Senate and the House in the election of 1946, and soon rallied around Senator Joseph McCarthy of Wisconsin. McCarthy characterized the Franklin Roosevelt-Harry Truman era as twenty years of treason. He recklessly claimed that there were 205 card-carrying communists in the State Department and eventually turned his investigative mania against an officer in the U.S. Army.

McCarthy's disgraceful conduct culminated in censure by the United States Senate. Thereafter he became a broken, tragic figure–a drunken isolate who went to an early grave.

Summary

Conservatives have always opposed progress and change, opting throughout our history to engage the electorate in distractions, and often making loyalty and character the dominant themes of their campaigns. In recent times a Republican-controlled Congress spent six valuable years investigating the public affairs and the private life of President Bill Clinton. A prominent scholar from Harvard Law School, Alan Dersowitch, labeled the lengthy investigation of Clinton's private life, an era of sexual McCarthyism.

In the George W. Bush administration, right wing zealots attacked big government. They were "in charge" of federal programs and agencies that they despised. Rules and regulations designed to enforce justice and fair play were ignored. After all, Bush's officials were chosen because they would not enforce regulations. Was the result a virtuous free market or a criminals' paradise?

There were also direct assaults on Social Security and Medicare. The call to privatize these programs was characterized as reform, but to the Democratic faithful, it was a blatant effort to destroy them.

There was also an indirect, long-term assault on the welfare state. That assault was deficit spending with its attendant accumulation of an enormous national debt. The time is rapidly approaching when the system will be incapable of sustaining Social Security, Medicare and other federal programs. If this trend is allowed to continue, the next generation will be asked to assume overwhelming tax burdens, paying basically the interest on a mountain of debt, with few, if any, benefits from federal programs.

In foreign affairs, Bush's appointee as United Nations Ambassador was hostile towards the U.N. Collective security, survival issues, and other momentous concerns received little or no attention in the George W. Bush administration.

III. Is Survival Possible?

Survival lies within the realm of human possibilities. But the window of opportunity is closing and will soon be shuttered.

If the earth is to be preserved for life as we know it, the United States must vigorously lead a movement to govern huge multinational corporations internationally. A world security system must soon be in place, as well, to protect the natural environment and control weapons of mass destruction.

Those who oppose polarization of governmental authority at the international level on grounds of practicality should be required to explain the practicality of allowing present trends in ozone depletion, acid rain, decimation of the rain forests, and global warming to go unabated or the proliferation of nuclear weapons to go unchecked.

Those who oppose governmental polarization of authority at the international level on the grounds of surrender of American freedom and national sovereignty should explore the possibilities of elevating the American system to the international level. If this could be done, without recourse to force or war, it would become the ultimate American triumph.

Self styled patriots of the right wing will not be a factor in elevating the American system. Nor will they be instrumental in promoting an ultimate American triumph. They will be vigorous obstructionists to the end.

The right wing loathes governmental power. They oppose every federal program that underwrites the prosperity of laborers, farmers, and the elderly. They lack social conscience and hate paying taxes in support of federal welfare programs. The central element of their approach under President Coolidge, President Reagan, and the two Bush Presidents was and is enormous tax cuts for the wealthy. Under Reagan and the two Bushes, this approach produced huge annual deficits and a mountain of national debt. The Obama administration inherited a national economic collapse and has been forced to add immense amounts to the deficit and the debt. It seems that with these trends, the day is fast approaching when the American people will be paying increased taxes just to keep up the interest on the national debt. When that day arrives federal credit will disappear along with any possibility that federal welfare programs can be maintained.

Conservative support for a modern industrial nation is minimal, and conservative faith in the American federal system should be ranked the least among us. Participation in the multilateral treaty known as the United Nations is without conservative support as well. It is truly ironic that while the Republican party of today is virtually pure in its conservative bent, the Republican candidate for President in 1940, Wendell Willkie wrote a book titled *One World*. Willkie praised the Russians and called for a world freed from colonialism and imperialism.

But in the world of today, conservative objections to the globalization of government and labor will be manifold. The arguments will center on assertions that such objectives are impossible, impractical, and naive. These assertions should prompt advocates of international programs to ask whether the present piecemeal approaches to planetary problems practical, sophisticated, or even remotely hopeful. At this stage of the discussion, the dialogue will usually deteriorate to the loyalty theme. Advocates of international labor and international government will be dubbed socialists and communists.

More thoughtful critics will correctly point out that support for world programs requires an altruistic spirit and attitudes that fly in the face of instinctive human behavior. They will assert that we are in the evolutionary process off taming the savagery that once included cannibalism; we are responding to tribal instincts that find modern fulfillment in the glorification of the nation-state; we sublimate our predatory nature and play at war as spectators and participants in violent contact sports; we paint our faces and whoop and scream in support of our sports heroes; we demand and receive violence on television, in the movies, and even in children's cartoons; and we know from experience that true survival means eliminating every threat, eliminating your competition, and dominating every adversary. These critics will say that even though we might conceptualize the urgent need for collective solutions—and even though we may discover new ego involvement and collective identity in the family of man—it will take a quantum leap and a transcendence of human nature to succeed in the quest to survive.

Many critics of collective security say that it is impossible to talk of a world security system until nations of the world are compatible philosophically and until a spirit of cooperation prevails. But if nations were compatible and harmonious, there would be no need for a world security system. It is precisely because the world is divided, fragmented, and dangerously close to nuclear and environmental destruction that a world security system is necessary.

Those who succumb to the many arguments against an international structure will shrink from the task. But perhaps large numbers of people will act on the belief that freedom will flourish when we modernize and strengthen the United Nations. The executive, legislative, and judicial branches could each be given limited and specific powers in a world constitution, thereby creating a system of checks and balances against tyranny. Liberty could grow and thrive if we create and enforce world laws that guarantee the freedoms found in the Universal Declaration of Human Rights. And 21st Century American pride could reign if a world system based on an American model were in place.

Chapter Two

Applying the System

IV. What is the Basic American System?

The American Federal Union is structured in a manner that harbors freedom, checks tyranny, encourages individual advancement, and allows change.

Our national government is separated into three distinct branches; namely, the executive, legislative and judicial. Our Constitution specifies the powers granted to each of these branches in a manner that creates separation of powers, checks and balances, and a very effective curb on tyranny in all branches of the national government. In addition the Constitution outlines a division of power between the national government and the states.

An Empowering Process

The Constitution also provides for a process of amendment. The American people have amended the Constitution twenty-seven times. The first ten amendments were added in the first days of our Republic. Collectively the first ten amendments are referred to as the Bill of Rights, a section of our Constitution in which personal freedoms are described and protected. In

Amendments 13, 14, and 15, we find, among other things, the abolition of slavery and the right to citizenship and suffrage for African-Americans. In the 17th Amendment power to elect U.S. Senators was removed from state legislatures and placed directly in the hands of the American people; the 19th Amendment gave the vote to American women, and the 23rd gave votes to residents of Washington, DC. The 26th Amendment granted citizens 18 year of age the right to vote

.

It is readily apparent that our Constitution harbors and anchors freedom, and through the process of amendment, it provides a vehicle for the elevation of debased minorities and needed changes of various kinds.

Guiding Principles

Many refer to "***In God We Trust***" as the United States motto, while others emphasize that it is "***E Pluribus Unum.***" In reality we have a dual motto. Each of these phrases appears on the money we exchange, but the latter appears on the obverse side of the Great Seal of the United States of America. This phrase translates into the English phrase "Out of Many, One." Nothing could be more appropriate in characterizing the multi-cultural, plural, and diverse society that comes together as one American nation.

On the reverse side of the Great Seal of the United States is a scroll bearing the inscription ***Novus Ordo Seclorum,*** which translates to "New Order of the Ages." The Latin phrases on each side of the Great Seal of the United States of America have universal applications and are indeed timeless.

V. Could the American Federal Union Serve as a Model for World Governance?

The significance of the American Federal Union is that it does provide a model for world governance. The freedom that is harbored and anchored in the American federal system can be harbored and anchored in a world federal system. If millions of acres of national forest reserve and national parks can be saved under the American federal system, the rainforests of the world can be saved under a world federal system. If a plural and diverse society can improve and progress under American federalism, a plural and diverse world society could progress under a world federal system. If separation of powers and checks and balances can check tyranny in the three branches of national government under the American federal system, the National Security Council, the General Assembly, and the International Court of Justice can be strengthened and encased in a system of checks and balances under world federalism. If justice, fair play, and human freedom can be enhanced on the national level through Supreme Court decisions based on the American Bill of Rights, justice, fair play, and human freedom can be enhanced by decisions of the World Court based on The Universal Declaration of Human Rights. And if domestic tranquility can be maintained under American federalism, the peace of the world can be insured through world federalism as well.

The inscriptions on the Great Seal of the United States of America are our guiding principles. In America we have striven for a society that is plural and diverse, and a society where many different kinds can live in safety, pursuing lives in which free choices abound.

Our task now, it seems, is to make the world a safe place in which free choices abound– in President Kennedy's words, to "make the world safe for diversity."

VI. What Are Some of the Conceivable Advantages of a World Federal System?

Imagine a World Constitution in place with a paraphrase of the Preamble to the United States Constitution. It might read:

We the people of the United Nations of the World, in order to form a more perfect union, establish justice, insure domestic tranquility, provide for the common defense, promote the general welfare, and secure the blessings of liberty to ourselves and our posterity, do ordain and establish this Constitution for the United Nations of the World.

Is it possible that this might be done? If Ambassador Eleanor Roosevelt could **inspire and lead** members of the United Nations to produce and ratify The Universal Declaration of Human Rights, which is a projection and an expansion of the freedoms contained in the American Bill of Rights, perhaps a World Constitution could be made with a preamble paraphrasing the goals of the American Federal Union.

Thermonuclear and environmental threats call for an agenda for world order.

But an agenda for world order takes courage, creativity and commitment. Heroic statesmen of World War II have left us with an American foundation for world law—three branches of international government and a magnificent Universal Declaration of Human Rights. Freedom's boundaries will expand and flourish when we modernize and strengthen the United Nations. A World Constitution can be fashioned on the American model, specifying limited powers for the Security Council, the General Assembly, and The International Court of Justice. Checks and balances can be fashioned to check tyranny on the world level, just as tyranny is checked in the American system. Judicial decisions by the International Court of Justice can be based on the Universal Declaration of Human Rights, just as judicial decisions of the U.S. Supreme Court are rooted in the American Bill of Rights. Freedom can and must be institutionalized now at the international level, and a world security system must be rendered in place to control nuclear weapons and curb environmental deterioration.

Major seats in the Security Council must now be given to Japan and Germany, and the crippling veto must be abolished, perhaps in favor of a substantial majority vote among the major powers, including Germany and Japan.

The dream of disarmament under enforceable world law could become a reality. A new world order could emerge in which peace dividends might enable nations of the world to replace massive spending for war with massive spending on infrastructures, improvements, and beautification,

In the United States, government contracts for internal improvements could be awarded on a competitive basis by a government agency as powerful as the Pentagon. Why shouldn't massive amounts of capital be diverted from war contracts and pumped into the rebuilding of America?

International corporations could be taxed and regulated in order to provide revenue for international projects and earth-friendly technology. If business corporations can expand worldwide, why not government as well? And why not labor organizations? An International labor movement could be developed to provide a counter force against powerful international corporations.

What remains of the rain forests of the world could be saved under a world federal system, just as Yellowstone, Yosemite, Bryce, Zion, the Grand Canyon, and millions of acres of forest reserve have been preserved under American federalism.

International assaults on environmental deterioration could be launched. Hydrogen and other non-polluting fuels could be promoted and developed internationally, just as American railroads, airlines, auto companies and farmers have been subsidized nationally.

Perhaps **non- polluting hydroelectric projects** such as the mammoth Tennessee Valley Authority, with its 35 huge dams along a 600-mile river system, could be developed internationally, and perhaps earth-friendly technology could be internationally subsidized throughout the world.

Heroes of the "Greatest Generation" conquered the Great Depression, won World War II, and left us with a solid foundation and a framework for survival. Can we accomplish the lesser part and build upon a great United Nations foundation to insure the peace and save the planet?

VII. Is There a Theoretical Basis for Promotion of the American System to the World Level?

Yes. An explanation of this affirmation lies in the evolution of social contract theory.

A Theoretical Basis for Hope

The theoretical foundation for the American Declaration of Independence and the Constitution lies in Social Contract theory. It was from the writings of John Locke, Thomas Hobbes, and Jean Jacques Rousseau that our founding fathers drew the rationale for the institutionalization of freedom and the practice of the consent of the governed.

Thomas Hobbes identified freedom as a natural condition for mankind, but he also explained that in our natural state, mankind had a "nasty," "brutish," and "short" life experience. Our primate progenitors, it seems, were free to rape, decapitate, cannibalize, and rely on a few savage kinsmen to assist in the struggle to survive.

A social contract emerged in this chaos. A clan of individuals tacitly agreed to surrender their freedom to commit savagery against one another. They set rules of conduct within their society. They began to institutionalize and protect positive freedoms, and they based decision-making on the consent of the governed. The clan, therefore, became the first political mechanism in the survival process, and the first institution to incorporate rudimentary ethical facets of modern civilization.

Clans evolved into tribes, where cooperation and bonding were strengthened through rules and laws, primitive religious rituals, symbols, and perhaps a flag. In this evolutionary process, mankind institutionalized freedom, developed a rule of law, and based decision-making on the consent of the governed.

As nomadic tribes became sedentary, rules for the village evolved into more sophisticated contracts, eventually culminating into city-states and thenceforth into modern nation-states. (1:73-74)

When Thomas Jefferson wrote our American creed–The Declaration of Independence–he characterized *freedom* as a gift from the Creator. He therefore *committed to the institutionalization of freedom* and other facets of the evolving social contract. Freedom, equality, and decision-making based on the consent of the governed were ideals that became the foundation for the new American nation.

The evolutionary social contract evolved into its most sophisticated manifestation in 1787, when American patriots rejected the anarchy and chaos they had experienced under the Articles of Confederation and created the Federal Union.

Are the conditions of the 21ˢᵗ Century nasty, brutish, and life threatening? Do they call for a universal social contract based on freedom, equality, a rule of law, and decision-making based on the consent of the governed?

Our rain forests are rapidly being destroyed. Shall we stand by while the lungs of the world are entirely ripped out? The hole in earth's protective ozone shield has grown larger than the continent of North America. Will we permit this to proceed? Do we intend to respond to the crisis of global warming? And what about numerous other environmental and thermonuclear trends that are equally urgent?

Is it time to create the ultimate social contract? Can we institutionalize freedom and save humanity by promoting a model of the American Federal Union as a political capstone over a battered and very tentative planet?

VIII. WHO ARE SOME OF THE ADVOCATES
OF A WORLD SECURITY SYSTEM?

President Roosevelt

Franklin D. Roosevelt said in a March 1, 1945, address to Congress that the United Nations Charter, which would be adopted in San Francisco, "will doubtless have to be amended time and time again over the years, just as our constitution has been . . ." (18:462-463)

Death stilled the voice of President Roosevelt on April 12, 1945, and in a speech to be delivered at the Jefferson Day Dinner on April 13, he was scheduled to say, "The only limit to our realization of tomorrow will be our doubts of today. Let us move forward with strong and active faith." (18:463)

The vision of FDR is needed in the new century. While many courageous leaders have called for the strengthening of the United Nations, the United Nations Charter has not been significantly changed since its inception in 1945.

Albert Einstein was a strong advocate of world government. *Einstein on Peace* is recommended reading. On February 19, 1950, he delivered an address on NBC television titled, "Peace in the Atomic Era."

Albert Einstein

In that address he said, "The first problem is to do away with fear and mistrust. Solemn renunciation of violence . . . is necessary. Such renunciation, however, can only be effective if at the same time a supra-national judicial and executive body is set up empowered to decide questions of immediate concern to the security of nations." (6:302) He also asserted "There is no salvation for civilization, or even the human race, other than the creation of a world government."

Edward Teller, Father of the Hydrogen Bomb, wrote in his book, *The Legacy of Hiroshima*, "Our goal in the final analysis, cannot be merely to do away with arms and armies. We must, instead, work for the elimination of irresponsible and illegal acts of independent nations. We must work for the establishment of a world authority sustained by moral force and physical force–a worldwide government capable of enforcing worldwide law and worldwide disarmament" (13:209)

Edward Teller

President Truman

Harry S. Truman said in his State of the Union Address, January 21, 1946, "The United Nations Organization now being established represents a minimum essential beginning . . . . Our ultimate security requires more than a process of consultation and compromise. It requires that we begin now to develop the United Nations organization as the representative of the world as one society." (12:39)

He also said, "It will be just as easy for nations of the world to get along in a republic of the world as it is for you to get along in the republic of the United States. Now when Kansas and Colorado have a quarrel over the water in the Arkansas River, they don't call out the National Guard in each state and go to war over it. They bring suit in the Supreme Court of the United States and abide by the decision. There isn't a reason in the world why we can't do that internationally."

President Eisenhower

Dwight D. Eisenhower called for the pursuit of world law on many occasions. In a letter written to Senator Hubert Humphrey, November 17, 1959, and later published in the *U.S. Department of State Bulletin*, January 25, 1950 v. 42, pp. 128-30, President Eisenhower said, "One of the great purposes of this administration is to advance the rule of law in the world, through actions directly by the United States government and in concert with the governments of other countries. It is open to us to further this great purpose both through optimum use of existing international institutions and through the adoption of changes and improvements in those institutions."

In this same letter, President Eisenhower advocated that the United States accept rulings and decisions of the International Court of Justice as binding on our country. He unequivocally called for the strengthening of the International Court of Justice and the development of world law.

In his Second Inaugural Address Eisenhower stated, "There must be law, steadily invoked and respected by all nations, for without law, the world promises only such meager justice as the pity of the strong upon the weak . . . . We recognize and accept our own deep involvement in the destiny of men everywhere. We are accordingly pledged to honor, and to strive to fortify, the authority of the United Nations. For in that body rests the best hope of our age for the assertion of that law by which all nations may live in dignity."

Hidden Hand and Indirect Leadership Style

While President Eisenhower was popularly identified as a cold warrior who used nuclear threats and brinkmanship, Fred Greenstein has helped us to understand his "hidden hand" presidency, with its attendant goal of ***Waging Peace,*** utilizing the tactics of threat, bluff, and an indirect leadership style.

Eisenhower threatened the use of nuclear weapons in Korea and bluffed his way to a quick truce. When Red China shelled Quemoy and Matsu, Eisenhower decided to avoid direct confrontation, to make confusing statements on China's actions, to test nuclear weapons in the Nevada desert, to stage air drills near the China coast, and to speak generally of the efficacy of employing nuclear weapons. His indirect approach frightened China into a ceasefire. Vice President Nixon later characterized Eisenhower's tactics as "devious in the best sense of the word."

In retrospect, it seems that Eisenhower's "bluff and brinkmanship" in foreign affairs has been validated. While threatening massive nuclear retaliation, he practiced judicious restraint and presided over two terms where there was no American involvement in war anywhere in the world.

Chief Justice Earl Warren

Earl Warren gave an address as Chief Justice of the United States, in Geneva Switzerland, on March 12,

1966. His message was "world peace through world law," a theme he stressed on other occasions as well." (16:387-390)

Arnold J. Toynbee was the internationally renowned British historian who repeatedly advocated world government. In the *New York Times Magazine*, April 5, 1964, he wrote a compelling article titled, "It is One World or No World." (14:28)

Norman Cousins was the editor of *Saturday Review* who wrote over a thousand editorials and essays about thermonuclear issues. He was an advocate of world federalism who made over two thousand advocacy speeches. He wrote many books calling for the development of world peace through world law. Among them were three compelling works; namely, 1) *Modern Man is Obsolete*, 2) *Who Speaks for Man?* and 3) *In Place of Folly*.

Norman Cousins

He was also Chairman of The National Committee for a Sane Nuclear Policy (SANE) and The World Federalist Association; and in the 1960s he became famous for facilitating communication between the Kremlin, the Vatican, and The White House. His work was highly instrumental in achieving the Nuclear Test Ban of 1963. This agreement banished the threat of radioactive fallout from atmospheric testing, worldwide. The story of his work on the nuclear test ban is chronicled in his book titled, *The Improbable Triumvirate*.

Norman Cousins received the personal medallion of Pope John XXIII. He was also the recipient of The Eleanor Roosevelt Peace Award in 1963, The Family of Man Award in 1968, and the United Nations Peace Medal in 1971. That he was never awarded the Nobel Peace Prize was an incredible oversight.

Walter Cronkite served as the anchor for CBS News for many years. He was often called "the most trusted man in America." His recent book, *A Reporter's Life: Walter Cronkite,* contains these perceptive words: "If we are to avoid that catastrophe (nuclear destruction), a system of world order—preferably a system of world government—

Walter Cronkite

is mandatory. The proud nations someday will see the light and for the common good and their own survival, yield up their precious sovereignty, just as America's thirteen colonies did two centuries ago." (5:128)

George H. W. Bush pursued an effective approach in foreign affairs which he called The New World Order. When confronted with Iraqi aggression against Kuwait, Bush organized a United Nations coalition that drew its authority from unanimous Security Council resolutions. This brilliant strategy curbed Iraqi aggression, contained Saddam Hussein, and left U.N. Inspectors in Iraq. The New World Order was morally correct. The entire world shared the costs and the risks, stopped aggression, and responded to a planned exit strategy. On April 13, 1991, Bush delivered an address at Maxwell Air

President Bush

Force Base in Montgomery, Alabama titled "The Possibility of a New World Order: Unlocking the Promise of Freedom." (4:450-452) George H. W. Bush made the United Nations work as it had never worked before or since.

John F. Kennedy was widely regarded as a hawk, a cold warrior, and the president who took us to the brink of nuclear war in the Cuban missile crisis. Missing in most historical and biographical accounts is JFK's unswerving dedication to the building of world peace through world law

President Kennedy

JFK described the power of nuclear weapons and warned the American people that they must be internationally controlled. From his salad days as a U.S. Senator to the hour of his death, he made heroic proposals for "a grand and global alliance, a strengthened United Nations, a world security system, world peace through the development of world law, and a worldwide program of conservation." (1) (2) (3)

It was on September 20, 1963, in an address before the U.N., that President Kennedy called for "a worldwide program of conservation (which) could protect the forest and wild game preserves now in danger of extinction for all time, improve the marine harvest from our oceans, and prevent the contamination of air and water by industrial as well as nuclear pollution." In the same address he warned us "that the effort to improve the conditions of man . . . is not a task for the few. It is the task of all nations . . ." (11:693-698)

These words are as current as today's headlines. Yet when JFK spoke them, the Santa Barbara oil spill and the beginning of environmental consciousness were more than five years away. Ozone depletion was not yet understood, the greenhouse effect and global warming were not yet identified, the rain forests were, for the most part, intact, acid rain was not yet ravaging the forests of Germany, Central Europe, Northeast United States, and Canada, and Earth Day had not yet been proclaimed. But JFK's proposal for "a worldwide program of conservation" was ignored then as it is ignored now.

In 2005, The World Resources Institute published statistics showing that logging and conversion have reduced the world's forests by 50%. Meanwhile, about 100 square miles of rain forest (the lungs of the world) are lost each day; and about ten thousand species of fish are threatened globally.

Mikhail Gorbachev, former premier of the Soviet Union, led his country through *glasnost* and *perestroika* to the abandonment of the Communist dictatorship. The August, 1992 issue of the *Bulletin of the Atomic Scientists,* contains a Gorbachev address delivered on May 6, 1992, at Westminster College in Fulton, Missouri. The title of this speech is "The River of Time," and it was delivered at the exact spot where Winston Churchill had delivered his famous "Iron Curtain" address forty-six years earlier. Gorbachev's theme was that Churchill's address helped open the cold war, and that the time had arrived for a new era.

Gorbachev said that Stalin was wrong for using the post WW II era as an opportunity to spread socialism. He also criticized Churchill and Truman for squandering the opportunity to build international order and stability through collective security. Gorbachev then called for a global security system to prevent nuclear war and to halt worldwide environmental deterioration. (8:22-24+)

IX. Which American Leader Gave the Most Support to the Development of a World Security System?

John F. Kennedy was the most dedicated of all advocates of world law. He first called for world law in two important speeches as a young Senator. As a candidate for the presidency, he and his New Frontiersmen charted a bold pathway when they developed the following plank in the

Democratic Party Platform of 1960:
The United Nations

To all of our fellow members of the United Nations:

We shall strengthen our commitments in this, our great continuing institution for conciliation and the growth of a world community. Through the machinery of the United Nations, we shall work for disarmament, the establishment of an international police force, the strengthening of the World Court, and the establishment of world law.

We shall propose the bolder and more effective use of the specialized agencies to promote the world's economic and social development. Great Democratic Presidents have taken the lead in the effort to unite the nations of the world in an international organization to assure world peace with justice under law.

The League of Nations, conceived by Woodrow Wilson, was doomed by Republican defeat of United States participation.

John F. Kennedy

The United Nations, sponsored by Franklin Roosevelt, has become the place where representatives of the rival systems and interests which divide the world can and do maintain continuous contact.

The United States adherence to the World Court contains a so-called "self-judging reservation" which in effect permits us to prevent a court decision in any particular case where we are involved. The Democratic Party proposes its repeal.

To all these endeavors so essential to world peace, We the members of the Democratic Party, will bring a new urgency, persistence and determination, born of the conviction that in our thermonuclear century all of the other Rights of Man hinge on our ability to guarantee man's right to peace. (17) (See also 1:4-5)

When JFK became president, the *New York Times* covered his inaugural with the front page banner headline

Kennedy Sworn In; Asks Global Alliance Against Tyranny, Want, Disease and War

JFK called for a "grand and global alliance" and the development of world law not only in his inaugural, but also in an address before the United Nations on September 25, 1961, in his remarks after signing the bill creating the new Arms Control and Disarmament Agency, in the Third State of the Union message, in a Commencement Address at American University on June 10, 1963, in a television address about the Nuclear Test Ban Treaty on July 26, 1963, and in his final address before the United Nations on September 20, 1963. (1,3).

President Kennedy was not intimidated by the John Birch society or other right wing extremists of his day. He looked across a world of threats and proposed "a grand and global alliance." He went to the United Nations just two months before his death and spoke with pride about how the Sixteenth and Seventeenth General Assemblies had reduced world tension; he reminded the delegates that the United Nations Decade of Development was successfully underway, and that a nuclear test ban treaty, banning atmospheric testing, had just been signed by over one hundred nations. He then said that his visit to the U.N. was not prompted by a crisis, but by confidence. "I have come to salute the United Nations and to show the support of the American people for your daily deliberations," he said. "The United Nations has made great progress, but more can be done.

A world center for health communications under the World Health Organization would warn of epidemics and the adverse effects of certain drugs, as well as transmit the results of new experiments and new discoveries.

Regional research centers could advance our common medical knowledge and train new scientists and doctors for new nations.

A global system of satellites could provide communication and weather information for all corners of the earth.

A worldwide program of conservation could protect the forest and wild game preserves now in danger of extinction for all time, improve the marine harvest of food from our oceans, and prevent the contamination of air and water by industrial as well as nuclear pollution." (11: 693-698)

Kennedy then praised the peace-keeping achievements of the United Nations "in the Congo, in the Middle East, in Korea and Kashmir, in West New Guinea and Malaysia. "But what the United Nations has done in the past is less important than the tasks for the future . . . ." he said and then proceeded to his most comprehensive rendition of a familiar theme.

The United Nations cannot survive as a static organization. Its obligations are increasing as well as its size. Its charter must be changed as well as its customs. The authors of that charter did not intend that it be frozen in perpetuity. The science of weapons and war has made us all, far more than eighteen years ago in San Francisco, one world and one human race, with one common destiny. In such a world absolute sovereignty no longer assures us of absolute security. The conventions of peace must pull abreast and then ahead of the conventions of war. The United Nations, building on its successes and learning from its failures, must be developed into a genuine world security system." (11:693-698)

Two days before his death, President Kennedy submitted the 17th Annual Report to the Congress on *U.S. participation in the United Nations*. He closed the document with these words. "But despite non-cooperation from some members, and wavering support from others, the organization has moved significantly toward the goal of a *peace system, worldwide in scope*. The United States will continue to lend vigorous support to the building of that system." (11:880-882)

Vigorous support for the building of that system died on November 22, 1963.

Compare the courage and vision of JFK with those who followed. Compare his words with those of our leaders of today.

Kennedy did arm his critics by advocating disarmament and arms buildup simultaneously He explained that we had to convince the Soviet Union that they could not win the arms race, but that we ultimately must look across this world of threats and build a safe, viable world, governed by law.

X. Who Are Some Other Americans Who Have Led in the Promotion of Peace and the Preservation of Our Environment?

President Wilson

Woodrow Wilson gave the world section one of the Treaty of Versailles. It was called the Covenant of the League of Nations. All nations that signed the Treaty of Versailles accepted membership in the League of Nations. Ironically the American President authored and fathered the League, but the United States Senate refused to ratify the treaty and accept membership.

In the ensuing years, isolationist America sat idly by and watched the Japanese expand in Asia while Nazi Germany dominated Western Europe. When Japan attacked the U.S., Isolationism was forever dead.

After the Americans, Russians, and British defeated the Rome-Berlin-Tokyo Axis, with smoke rising from three blood-stained continents, with the dawn of the atomic era, the United States Senate accepted membership in the United Nations with a smashing vote of 89 to 2. President Wilson was thus vindicated for his wisdom and foresight. He is one of the four American Presidents who have received the Nobel Prize.

Eleanor Roosevelt made an enormous contribution to world peace and understanding as Ambassador to the United Nations. Widely admired as a former First Lady of the United States, she soon became known as First Lady of the World.

At the United Nations she became the Chairperson of the Commission that drafted the Universal Declaration of Human Rights. If James Madison can be recognized as The Father of the American

Eleanor Roosevelt

Bill of Rights, Eleanor Roosevelt must be referred to as the leader who re-framed those rights and obtained their ratification in the General Assembly of the United Nations. The hope for survival of mankind, in a world of freedom, justice, and peace, depends upon the swift codification of these ideals into enforceable world law. The Universal Declaration of Human Rights can be found in the appendices of this book.

President Jimmy Carter's contributions in the promotion of human rights have been outstanding. As President he held all nations accountable for violations of human rights, boycotting the Moscow Olympics and using other means to remind the nations of their commitment to the Universal Declaration of Human Rights. He stands in bold relief in the pantheon of highly visible practicing Christians, in that he is indeed a doer of the word. That his Carter Center is continually involved in resolving world problems is well known. President Carter is one of only four presidents to receive the Nobel Peace Prize.

President Carter

Ted Turner, former broadcast mogul, is the most compassionate and generous of all the entrepreneurs. No living person has exceeded his effort in the promotion of peace and environmental goals.

For many years he sponsored and financed the Goodwill Games that helped to thaw the chill of the cold war. He has purchased $500 million worth of land with the primary purpose of conserving and preserving species. Turner's commitment to all living things honors Albert Schweitzer's oft quoted phrase, "reverence for life." He has given $1 billion dollars to the United Nations and set up a U.N. foundation to handle the disbursements. He has established and financed a Nuclear Threat Initiative which has done impressive work in reducing the threat of nuclear, biological and radiological weapons. And in addition to all of this, his Turner foundation promotes environmental causes.

CHAPTER THREE
Overcoming the Obstacles

XI. WILL AMERICAN MEDIA DISCOURAGE THE DEVELOPMENT OF PROGRAMS OF COLLECTIVE SECURITY?

Yes. Indeed the media will. The American media, both print and electronic, has passed into the hands of a few giant corporations. There will be little or no support for programs of collective security, not only because powerful commercial interests own the media, but also because they are in no way compelled to present viewpoints that are deemed inimical to corporate interests.

XII. AREN'T RADIO AND TELEVISION STATIONS REQUIRED TO AIR VARIOUS POINTS OF VIEW?

No they are not. In America we have already experienced the death of fair speech. An account of how this happened follows:

In 1949 The Federal Communications Commission spoke of all radio and television stations as "public trustees" that had an obligation to seek out issues of public importance and air all points of view. This was the essence of the so-called Fairness Doctrine.

In ensuing years the FCC laid out rules prohibiting personal attack and political editorializing. The FCC also required that as part of their license renewal application, stations had to report their efforts to seek out and address issues of concern to the community.

And then came President Reagan. As the first conservative president since Calvin Coolidge, he announced his Reagan Revolution– a sweeping attempt to reduce the federal government and return power to the states.

Mark Fowler, Reagan's appointee to the Federal Communications Commission, firmly believed in destroying the federal government's power to regulate. He publicly announced that he would kill the Fairness Doctrine. He cleared the pathway for this action when the FCC sued the League of Women Voters and the U.S. Supreme Court came up with its curious decision in 1984 that the Fairness Doctrine ". . . inescapably dampens the vigor and limits the variety of public debate." In this same case the Court also explained that when the Fairness Doctrine was used, there were only a few big networks that could easily monopolize opinion. By comparison, in the 1980s there were so many avenues of news that diversity was a natural part of the news and opinion landscape. This interpretation is thoroughly flawed in the new century where both electronic and print media has fallen into the hands of a few giant corporations.

At any rate, Mark Fowler got the Supreme Court Decision he sought and immediately laid down the FCC ruling that the Fairness Doctrine was dead, because we had diversity of opinion without federal regulation. He also asserted that the Fairness Doctrine inhibited the presentation of controversial issues.

Congress angrily passed legislation reinstating the Fairness Doctrine. In the House of Representatives the law passed with a 3-to-1 margin. It also passed in the Senate at a ratio of nearly 2 to 1. The law even got the support of Newt Gingrich in the House and Jesse Helms in the Senate. But President Reagan smiled amiably, vetoed the legislation, and opened the cruel, treacherous pathway to the death of American fair speech.

In 1989 Congress revived the fairness issue and the Fairness Doctrine Bill easily passed the House again. But it soon bogged down when President Bush threatened to veto it. Hearings were held on the bill in 1991, but George Herbert Walker Bush quashed the effort again.

Since that time it is possible for radio talk show hosts to engage in endless tirades without any responsibility on the part of the host or the station to present an opposite point of view. It is possible, therefore, to employ a no-guest format, shriek at the four walls, and reverberate in millions of homes and automobiles in a most totalitarian way.

While corporate control of the airways has smothered commitment to balance or American fair play on any of our radio or television stations, there is one redeeming factor in all this. Since about 2005, MSNBC, a cable TV station, began featuring liberal, leftist comment. There is now more choice and better balance between the conservative right and the liberal left.

XIII. Why is the American Federal Union a Model for World Governance?

One of the objections raised against the establishment of world government is that we must all subscribe to the same ideology in order to make it work. The truth of the matter is that if the world were ideologically in lock-step, it would probably have little need for a system of world governance.

The world we live in, however, is religiously, ideologically, politically, economically, socially, and culturally fragmented. We are dangerously divided with the technological capacity to end all life. Circumstances in the world cry incessantly for order, stability, and safety.

The American Federal Union is a model for world governance because under a magnificent umbrella of freedom, it has embraced pluralism and diversity. The American system accommodates differences in religion, politics, and races. American federalism is not perfect, but it offers the best possible structure for a successful world security system. Abraham Lincoln issued prophetic words for our time when he said, "My dream is of a place and time where America will once again be seen as the last best hope on earth."

XIV. What Steps Can Be Taken to Create a Safe American World?

The first and most important step is to rid ourselves of the policy of preemptive war against potential nuclear nations. This approach betrays American ideals and surrenders any claim our nation can make to moral leadership.

As a prelude to World War II, the Rome-Berlin-Tokyo Axis conducted savage aggression in the Middle East, Europe, and Asia. British, United States and Soviet armed forces destroyed the perpetrators of violence who glorified force and practiced aggression.

After World War II, President Truman organized an international police force to contain North Korean aggression. The United Nations contained North Korea and preserved the government of South Korea, and The United States was honored throughout the free world as a great world power that would take a stand against aggression.

In Korea, the United States became the champion of containment and a strong advocate of collective security, with the goal of sustaining international order and upholding international law. This was indisputably congruent with the highest of moral principles.

In Vietnam, President Lyndon Johnson abandoned the principle of collective security and conducted an ill-defined mission, without allies and without success. Nevertheless, our effort in Vietnam, it seems, was to contain North Vietnamese aggression, and not to wage aggressive war.

George Herbert Walker Bush demonstrated enlightened leadership in "Desert Storm." He was squarely on the side of collective security and the pursuit of international order. His New World Order was an enormous success in terms of organizational structure. Arabs and Jews, capitalists and communists, and every other improbable combination joined hands to stop the Iraqi invasion of Kuwait. The mission was clearly defined and the whole world understood it. The authority for the mission came from unanimous U.N. Security Council resolutions. Casualties were minimal, the costs of the operation were shared by all nations, and they pale by comparison to the costs of our present involvement in Iraq. Aggression was contained and U.N. inspection teams were left in Iraq.

George W. Bush recklessly abandoned the principles of collective security and the ideal of international order. He believed that U. S. interests were best served by attacking nations that his team identified as an imminent threat. The invasion of Iraq was conducted with a "coalition of the willing," which readily dissipated; and the military involvement in Iraq continued on after the much heralded announcement of "mission accomplished."

George W. Bush operated with a much discredited model which has been historically associated with America's enemies, not her friends. Much damage was done to American prestige under his administration. The NATO free world defense shield is in disarray. We have destroyed the trust, the good will and the cooperation among members of the United Nations. It will be very difficult to rebuild what we once had.

We have also lost valuable time in the implementation of a survival perspective. In the thermonuclear age the world is becoming more battered, more environmentally challenged, and more tentative with each passing day. In the future, the building of a viable world can be no part- time commitment. It will never be achieved without consistent dedication and the persistent work of an informed citizenry.

In the meantime, how can an American triumph be defined in Iraq? Why are Americans in Iraq? Was the Bush administration dedicated to the spread of liberty? Was it anxious to export democracy? Or did Bush intend to dominate this portion of the earth for exploitation and economic gain?

There was much rhetoric about the liberation of Iraq and the planting of the flag of liberty. With the holding of free elections in Iraq we gave more credence to these claims. But there are lingering doubts. What did the building of American bases in Iraq mean? Will Iraq truly be liberated or will it become a U.S. satellite? Is it important for the U.S. to dominate the Middle East for economic gain?

Project 2025: A Proposal

There is much to ponder as the new generation comes of age. Every American should actively participate in the shaping of the next quarter century. The alternative is a horror-filled drift toward oblivion.

Can we designate the year 2025 as the finish line? Can we set a survival agenda for the first quarter of the new century and implement it?

The Survival Hot List outlines some general objectives for our future. These objectives focus on the international resolution of *The Seven Deadly Trends* through the development of world law.

Those who believe that these objectives lack merit should specify and promote their own visions of hope. Many on the religious right have suggested that catastrophe is inevitable and that the earth will be purged of the wicked. In the meantime, nothing should be done to attempt to alter a divine plan. President Kennedy, by contrast, closed his inaugural with words that indicated his belief that catastrophe can be averted. He said, "With a good conscience our only sure reward, with history the final judge of our deeds, let us go forth to lead the land we love, asking His blessing and His help, but knowing that here on earth God's work must truly be our own."

What say you? It would be fascinating if a number of individuals and groups could compete in the marketplace of ideas under an umbrella called Project 2025. One possibility is that a massive religious movement called the Peacemakers could be organized. There is an enormous scriptural rationale for such a movement that could be extracted from all great world religions. Who will organize an international movement of faith called the Peacemakers? Christian scripture identifies the peacemakers as the children of God. Perhaps the Peacemakers could be developed on the worldwide web.

The internet would seem to be an ideal place for the development and promotion of various other survival perspectives as well. Student designed "Model Declarations of Interdependence" could compete for recognition. If they were presented in the form of petitions, provisions for the public to sign on could be made. Perhaps a vigorous dialogue could be commenced on President John F. Kennedy's proposed Grand and Global Alliance and President George H. W. Bush's proposed New World Order.

Project 2025 could promote the development of a number of university-sponsored Model United Nations Conferences with a focus on student involvement in U.N. charter review. The essential question would seem to be: How can we convert a multilateral treaty known as the United Nations into a permanent peace-keeping structure and an institution to curb environmental deterioration?

Project 2025 could be developed in the classroom by instructors with courage and vision. Social scientists could involve students in the pursuit of a genuine *survival agenda*. The examination of alternative futures could foster a new, creative, academic environment. New curriculum could give added credence to departments called social "science," and bring relevance to their syllabi and hope to young lives.

Project 2025 could become an important part of the work at the Carter Center. President Carter's worldwide crusade for human rights could be expanded. Worldwide conferences could explore strategies for implementing the Universal Declaration of Human Rights and promoting the development of world law. President Carter's work in the area of alternative fuels could also be expanded to promote the use of renewable energy and appropriate technology.

Project 2025 could enlist the John F. Kennedy School of Government, at Harvard University, in an effort to explore the legacy of the JFK presidency. His inaugural, the major portion of which deals with the issues of peace, international cooperation, and world law, should be publicly analyzed. Kennedy's numerous speeches and statements about the need to strengthen the United Nations and create a world security system and a worldwide program of conservation should be publicly examined. The scheduling of public forums on JFK's role as a spokesman for our new century is an urgent matter.

Project 2025 could enlist the support of public figures for public lectures and discussions on JFK's Grand and Global Alliance at the John F. Kennedy Presidential Library. Nothing could be more appropriate or more vital in the august atmosphere of this great institution.

Project 2025 could become a blog on the worldwide web—an umbrella where a variety of peace proposals could be presented and discussed.

Project 2025 could be an organized effort, stressing time-sensitive issues. The year 2025 could become the finish line when survival machinery must be in place. Otherwise the year 2025 will likely become a finish line of a different kind. The time is rapidly approaching when our window of opportunity will be shuttered. The rainforests will be depleted; the protective ozone, the polar ice caps, and all life sustaining elements will be eroded or perhaps destroyed by thermonuclear means.

Project 2025 could promote the wide dissemination of a Resolution of Interdependence. Carefully peruse the Resolution of Interdependence, which is presented as a petition. If you are so inclined, please sign this petition which could be presented to the President and our representatives in Congress.

XV. What Could Be Called the Ultimate American Triumph?

Often cited as the motto of The United States of America, E Pluribus Unum appears on the obverse side of The Great Seal of the United States of America, and upon the currency we exchange in our daily business transactions. This motto translates into the English phrase, "Out of Many, One." Unity in pluralism and diversity is a magnificent American ideal which stands as a unique model for world governance. On the reverse side of the Great Seal is a scroll bearing the words Novus Ordo Seclorum, which translates to "New Order of the Ages." These phrases on our Great Seal have universal applications and are indeed timeless.

The ultimate American triumph could occur when American federalism is in place as a worldwide structure of governance. Specifically this could mean worldwide institutionalization of freedom with built- in curbs against tyranny. The following Resolution of Interdependence illustrates this concept:

The Resolution of Interdependence
Conquering the Seven Deadly Trends

A Call to Conquer the Seven Deadly Trends
Through the Strengthening of the United Nations
And the Development of World Law

To the President of the United States and Members of Congress:

We the undersigned, petition the President of the United States and members of Congress to support a vigorous international effort to conquer the seven deadly trends, which are 1) the thermonuclear threat to all life on earth, 2) destruction of rain forests, 3) global warming, 4) ozone depletion, 5) acid rain, 6) population explosion, and 7) all forms of military aggression.

We urge the swift reinstatement of the foreign policy approach of great American Presidents who stressed the need for collective security in foreign affairs. Among them were Woodrow Wilson, Franklin D. Roosevelt, Harry S. Truman, Dwight D. Eisenhower, John F. Kennedy and George Herbert Walker Bush.

President Woodrow Wilson was the Father of the League of Nations, and in a very real sense the Father of the United Nations.

President Franklin D. Roosevelt worked tirelessly to establish the United Nations and then admonished us to change and adapt it to new times.

John F. Kennedy called for the development of world law in speeches as a Senator on December 11, 1959 and on June 14, 1960, and as President in his Inaugural Address, in an address before the United Nations on September 25, 1961, in remarks after signing the bill creating the Arms Control and Disarmament Agency on September 26, 1961, in his Third State of the Union message on January 14, 1963, in his commencement address at American University on June 10, 1963, and in his last address at the United Nations on September 20, 1963, where he also proposed a worldwide program of conservation.

While President Kennedy was the most dedicated and persistent leader in the fight to strengthen the United Nations and develop world law, President Truman called for the strengthening of the United Nations in his State of the Union Address, July 26, 1946. He also organized a United Nations police force that protected the sanctity of the Republic of Korea and contained North Korean aggression.

President Eisenhower called for the development of "a world community under law," and the strengthening of The International Court of Justice.

Calling his foreign policy approach The New World Order, President George H.W. Bush organized the whole world in opposition to Iraqi aggression against Kuwait.

We the undersigned oppose the radical departure in foreign affairs under George W. Bush. The practice of preemptive first strike has furnished an example that, if followed by other nations, can only break down trust and international order. Furthermore, it has weakened the United Nations and our traditional free world alliances and destroyed our moral authority throughout the world.

We ask that the people of all nations join us in an effort to **conquer the seven deadly trends** described in the Resolution of Interdependence that follows. We have signed this petition to be sent with the Resolution of Interdependence as a working paper for the President of the United States and members of Congress.

The Resolution of Interdependence
CONQUERING THE SEVEN DEADLY TRENDS

Origin: Joseph A. Bagnall
Submitted by: Joseph A. Bagnall

WHEREAS, the seven deadly trends are 1) the thermonuclear threat to all life, 2) destruction of rain forests, 3) global warming, 4) ozone depletion, 5) acid rain, 6) population explosion, and 7) all forms of military aggression, and

WHEREAS, the seven deadly trends have been identified and defined, and if they are not resolved internationally, they will rapidly destroy civilization as we know it, and

WHEREAS, unregulated and uncontrolled nuclear weapons will eventually destroy our planet, and

WHEREAS, destruction of rain forests is altering life-sustaining atmospheric conditions and threatening to radically change earth's climate, and

WHEREAS, man-made gasses are polluting the atmosphere, creating greenhouse gasses that in turn create a canopy effect that produces global warming, which in turn is melting the earth's glaciers and polar ice caps and will inevitably threaten earth's shorelines and alter the world map, and

WHEREAS, man-made gasses have torn earth's protective ozone shield and created, according to NASA, a hole larger than the North American Continent, and

WHEREAS, destruction of earth's protective ozone layer will result in severe damage to all forms of life, and

WHEREAS, acid rain is rapidly destroying lakes and forests, chiefly in Northeastern United States, Canada, and Europe and has been destructive of many monuments and statuary in our world, and

WHEREAS, population explosion brings attendant environmental and political problems worldwide, and

WHEREAS, all forms of military aggression break down international order and pose the possibility of escalation into nuclear war, and

WHEREAS, deadly environmental and thermonuclear trends call for the enforcement of collective remedies, and

WHEREAS, great American Presidents such as Dwight D. Eisenhower and John F. Kenned, great American jurists such as Chief Justice Earl Warren, great American journalists such as Walter Cronkite, and great American scientists such as Albert Einstein and Edward Teller **have all called for solutions to world problems through the development of world law, and**

WHEREAS, the great British historian, Arnold Toynbee has called for one world and the collective choice of life over death, and

WHEREAS, former Soviet leader Michael Gorbachev has called for a world security system to halt war and curb environmental deterioration, and

WHEREAS, Pope John XXIII has issued an Encyclical titled, Pacem in Terris, in which he praised the United Nations and The Universal Declaration of Human Rights, adding that he looked forward to the day when there is "a judicial and political ordering of the world community . . . when every human being can find in this organization (the U.N.) an effective safeguard of his personal rights . . . ," and

WHEREAS, President Harry S. Truman has protected the sanctity of the 38th parallel and the Republic of Korea with a United Nations stand against North Korean aggression, and

WHEREAS, President George Herbert Walker Bush has furnished the world with an excellent model of collective security when his "New World Order" curbed Iraqi aggression against Kuwait and left U.N. inspection teams in place in Iraq, and

WHEREAS, it now seems important to create a permanent world security system based on a common and widely utilized political structure, and

WHEREAS, many nations are governed under federal systems, including the former Soviet Union, the United States, Canada, Australia, and others, it seems that a federal system should be considered for world governance, and

WHEREAS, the American federal system has survived the transition from agricultural to industrial society, the challenge of civil war, many economic crises, and two devastating world wars, and

WHEREAS, the American federal system has emerged in the 21st Century as the structure of the super power of the world, and

WHEREAS, the American federal system has protected wildlife and millions of acres of national forest reserves and set aside many national parks, and

WHEREAS, the American federal system has provided a framework for the elevation and enfranchisement of debased minorities, and

WHEREAS, the American federal system has institutionalized freedom and harbored ideological differences and debate, and

WHEREAS, the American federal system has fostered pluralism and diversity in ethnicity and religion, and

WHEREAS, the American federal system has curbed tyranny with a system of checks and balances between three separate branches of American government, and

WHEREAS, the American Supreme Court has rendered decisions based on the ideals of the American Bill of Rights, and

WHEREAS, America's federal system features an effective division of power between the national government and the states, and

WHEREAS, American federalism has furnished subsidies, incentives, and contracts to private companies for the development of federal highways, railroads, airlines and various other national improvements, and

WHEREAS, the creation of a world federal system based on the model of the American federal system would be the ultimate American triumph, now, therefore, we the undersigned highly

RESOLVE, to work for the development of a world federal system patterned after the American model; and be it also

RESOLVED, that this world federal system should:

1. protect its rainforests, its wildlife, and its oceans, just as the American federal system has protected its wildlife and millions of acres of national forests and national parks;

2. provide a framework for the elevation of debased minorities, just as the American system has accommodated the elevation and enfranchisement of debased minorities;

3. promote and implement the ideals of the Universal Declaration of Human Rights, just as the American system has promoted and implemented the ideals in the American Bill of rights;

4. base the decisions of the International Court of Justice on the ideals expressed in the Universal Declaration of Human Rights, just as the decisions of the American Supreme Court are based on the ideals expressed in the American Bill of Rights;

5. foster and maintain a climate of pluralism and diversity, in the tradition of the American system;

6. curb tyranny with separation of powers and checks and balances between a strengthened Security Council, General Assembly, and The International Court of Justice, just as tyranny is curbed in the American system with a system of separation of powers and checks and balances between the executive, legislative, and judicial branches;

7. divide power between world authority and national authority, just as power is divided in the American system between the national government and the states;

8. furnish subsidies, incentives, and contracts to private companies for the development of alternatives to destructive fossil fuels throughout the world, just as subsidies, incentives and contracts have been given to private companies for various national projects in the United States; and

9. regulate international corporations for the welfare of mankind, just as corporations have been regulated by the United States Government, and be it also

RESOLVED, that we do denounce force and military aggression in favor of actions based on the consent of the governed, as we involve the people of the world in the building of a world federal system patterned after the American model, and be it finally

RESOLVED, that we the undersigned agree to promote this Resolution of Interdependence with a sense of utmost urgency, born of the conviction that thermonuclear and environmental trends could end civilization in the 21st Century.

Sincerely,

The Undersigned

Documentation - End Notes

(1)   Bagnall, Joseph A. *The Kennedy Option: Pursuit of World Law.* University Press of America, 2002.

(2)   _____, The Politics of Survival: Resolving the Seven Deadly Trends. McGraw-Hill, 1997.

(3)   _____.President John F. Kennedy's Grand and Global Alliance: World Order for the Century. University Press of America, 1992.

(4)   Bush, George Herbert Walker. "The Possibility of a New World Order." *Vital Speeches of the Day,"* May 15, 1991.

(5)   Cronkite, Walter. *A Reporter's Life: Walter Cronkite.* Alfred A. Knopf, 1997.

(6)   Einstein, Albert. "Peace in the Atomic Era," *Vital Speeches of the Day.* March 1, 1950.

(7)   _____Einstein on Peace. Simon and Schuster, 1960.

(8)   Gorbachev, Mikhail. "The River of Time," *The Bulletin of the Atomic Scientists,* Jl/Ag, 1992.

(9)   Public Papers of the Presidents of the United States: Dwight David Eisenhower, Containing the Messages, Speeches, and Statements of the President of the United States, January 1, 1960 to January 20, 1961. Washington, D.C.: U. S. Government Printing Office

(10) Public Papers of the Presidents of the United States: John F. Kennedy, Containing the Messages, Speeches, and Statements of the President, January 20, to December 31. 1961. Washington, D.C.: U.S. Government Printing Office, 1962.

(11)   Public Papers of the Presidents of the United States: John F. Kennedy. Containing the Messages, Speeches and Statements of the President, January 1, to November 22, 1963. Washington, D..C.: U.S. Government Printing Office, 1964.

(12)   Public Papers of the Presidents of the United States: Harry S. Truman, Containing the Messages, Speeches, and Statements of the President, January 1, to December 31, 1946. Washington, D.C.: U. S. Government Printing Office, 1962.

(13)   Teller, Edward. *The Legacy of Hiroshima*. Doubleday and Company, 1962.

(14)   Toynbee, Arnold J. "It is One World or No World," *New York Times Magazine*. April 5, 1964. See also "Conditions of Survival" *Saturday Review*. August 29, 1964, pp. 24-26+.

(15)   U. S. Congressional Record: Proceedings and Debates of the 86th congress, Second Session, Vol. 106, part 10, June 14, 1960 to June 22, 1960. Washington, D. C.: U. S.. Government Printing Office, 1960.

(16)   Warren, Earl. "World Peace through Law," *Vital Speeches of the Day*, April 15, 1966.

(17)   Wooley, John and Gerhard Peters. www.presidency.ucsb.edu/ Documents. Party Platforms. Democratic 1960. Excerpt of Plank on the United Nations.

(18)   Zevin, Ben. (Ed.) Nothing to Fear: The Selected Addresses of Franklin D. Roosevelt, 1932- 1945. Popular Library, 1962.

Bibliography

Books

Anderson, Anthony B. *Alternatives to Deforestation*. Columbia University Press, 1994.

Aron, Raymond L. *Theories of Nuclear Strategy*. New York: Doubleday, 1965.

Bolin, Bert. A comparative History of Social Responses to Climate Change: Ozone Depletion and Acid Rain. Massachusetts Institute of Technology Press, 2000.

Brower, Michael. *Cool Energy: the Renewable Solution to Global Warming*. Cambridge, Massachusetts: Union of Concerned Scientists, 1990.

Clark, Grenville and Louis B. Sohn. *World Peace through World Law*. Harvard University Press, 1973.

Commoner, Barry, et al, *Alternative Technologies for Power Production*, New York: Macmillan Information, 1975.

_____, *Making Peace with the Planet*, with bibliography. New York: Pantheon Books, 1990.

_____, *Toward a Livable World…* Massachusetts Institute of Technology Press, 1987.

_____, *Who Speaks for Man?* New York: Macmillan, 1953

Douglas, Scott. et al., *The Spread of Nuclear Weapons: A Debate*. Norton, 1998.

Ehrlich, Paul R. Extinction: *The causes and Consequences of the Disappearance of Species.* New York: Random House, 1981.

_____, and Anne H. Ehrlich. *The Population Explosion.* New York: Simon and Schuster, 1990.

_____, and Richard L. Harriman. *How to be a Survivor.* New York: Ballantine Books, 1971.

_____, *The Population Bomb.* New York: Ballantine Books, 1968.

_____, *The Science of Ecology.* New York: Macmillan, 1987.

Einstein, Albert. *Einstein on Peace.* New York: Simon and Schuster, 1960

Ellerman, A. Denny, et al., *Markets for Clean Air: The U.S. Acid Rain Program.* Cambridge University Press, 2000.

Elliot, Richard. *Ozone Diplomacy: New Directions in Safeguarding the Planet.* Harvard University Press, 1997.

Faminow, Merle B. *Cattle, Deforestation, and Development in the Amazon,* Oxford University Press, 1998.

Firor, John. *The Changing Atmosphere: A Global Challenge.* Yale University Press, 1992

Gardner, John F. *The Secret of Peace and the Environmental Crisis.* New York: Myrin Institute, 1978.

Gore, Al. Earth in the Balance: *Ecology and the Human Spirit.* Houghton Mifflin, 1992.

Harvey, Danny. *Global Warming: The Hard Science.* Prentice Hall, 1999.

Hocking, Collin, et al., *Global warming and the Greenhouse Effect.* University of California, Berkeley, Lawrence Hall of Science, 1999.

_____, *Acid Rain.* University of California, Berkeley, Lawrence Hall of Science, 1999.

Hoffman, Bruce. *Inside Terrorism*. Columbia University Press, 1999.

Hoffman, Peter. *The Forever Fuel: The Story of Hydrogen*. Boulder, Colorado: Westview Press, 1981.

Houghton, J.T.T. et al., *Global Warming: The Complete Briefing*. Cambridge University Press, 1997.

Kennedy, John F. *The Strategy of Peace*. New York: Harper, 1960.

Kennedy, Robert F. *To Seek a Newer World*. New York: Doubleday, 1968.

Leggett, Jeremy K. *Global Warming: The Greenpeace Report*. Oxford University Press, Inc., 1990. Lesser, Ian, et al., *Countering the New Terrorism*. Rand Corporation, 1999.

Lippman, Morton. *Chemical Contamination in the Human Environment*. New York: Oxford University Press, 1979.

Miller, Morris. *Debt and Environment, Converging Crises*. New York: United Nations, 1991.

Mylorie, Laurie. *Study of Revenge: Saddam Hussein's Unfinished War Against America*. American Enterprise Institute for Public Policy, 2000.

Nordhaus, W.D. and Joseph Boyer. *Warming the World: Economic Models of Global Warming*. Massachusetts Institute of Technology Press, 2000.

Peters, Robert L. and Thomas E. Lovejoy. *Global Warming and Biological Diversity*. Yale University Press, 1994.

Pillar, Paul R. *Terrorism and U.S. Foreign Policy*. Brookings Institution Press, 2001.

Riggs, John A. and Roger W. Sant. *After Kyoto: Are there Rational Pathways to a Global Sustainable Energy System?* Aspen Institute for Humanistic Studies, 1998.

Reich, Walter. Origins of Terrorism: Psychologies, Ideologies, Theologies, States of Mind. Woodrow Wilson Center Press, 1998.

Schell, Jonathon. *The Fate of the Earth*. Morrow, 1982.

_____, *The Fate of the Earth and the Abolition*. Stanford University Press, 1999.

Scientific Assessment of Ozone Depletion, 1998. UN Environment Programme, 1998.

Schlesinger, Arthur M., Jr. *A Thousand Days: John F. Kennedy in the White House*. New York: Houghton Mifflin, 1965.

Sorenson, Theodore C. *Kennedy*. New York: Harper, 1965.

Stern, Jessica. *The Ultimate Terrorists*. Harvard University Press, 2000

Victor, David. The Collapse of the Kyoto Protocol and the Struggle to Slow Global Warming. Princeton University Press, 2001.

Welner, Jonathon. *Planet Earth*. New York: Bantam Books, 1986.

_____, The Next One Hundred Years: Shaping the Fate of Our Living Earth, New York: Bantam Books, 1991.

American Advocates of World Law

Acheson, D.G. "Law and the Growth of the Institutional Community," *U.S. Department of State Bulletin*, 26:694 - 698 My 5'52.

_____, " Revamping the U.N. to Meet Aggression, "*U.S. News and World Report*, 29:60 - 63. S 26 ' 50.

Byrne, James F. "U.S. Views on Charter Review," *U.S. Department of State Bulletin*, 29:649 - 650 N 9 '53.

Clark, G. "Need for Total Disarmament under Enforceable World Law," *Current History*, 47:93:96 Ag '64

Cousins, Norman. "What is World Law?" *Saturday Review*, 48:24 - 25 Ag 14 '65.

Dulles, J. F. "Revision of U.N. Charter" *U.S. Department of State Bulletin,* 29:343 S 14 '53.

_____, "U.N. Charter Obsolete from the Start," *U.S. News and World Report,* (September 4, 1953), 35:89 - 91 S 4 '53.

_____, "What the U.N. Is and Might Be," *New York Times Magazine,* p.10, O 24 '48.

Einstein, Albert "Peace in the Atomic Era," *Vital Speeches,* 16:302 Mr 1 '50.

Eisenhower, Dwight D. and Richard Nixon. "Should U.S. Support World Law?" *Foreign Policy Bulletin,* 38:132 My 15 '59.

_____, "President Expresses Views on World Court and Disarmament," exchange of letters between D.D. Eisenhower and H.H. Humphrey, with bibliography, *U.S. Department of State Bulletin,* 42: 128 - 130 Ja 25 '60.

Finletter, T.K. "Timetable for World Government" *Atlantic,* 177:53 - 60 Mr '46.

Fleming, D.F. "Eisenhower's Quest for Peace," *Nation,* 191:521 - 525 D 31.

Fulbright, J.W. "Outlook for Peace: Sovereignty Must Give Way to Law,' *Vital Speeches,* 12:358 - 360 Ap 1 '46.

Goldberg, Arthur J. "Coming of Age of the U.N., " *U.S. Department of State Bulletin,* 55:492 - 496 O 3 '66.

_____, "Rule of Law in an Unruly World," U.S. Department of State Bulletin, 54:936 - 944 Je 13 '66.

Herter, Christian A. The Rule of Law among Nations,"with bibliography. *U.S. Department of State Bulletin,* 37:223 - 228 Ag 5 '57.

_____, and W.P. Rogers, "Self Judging Aspect of the U.S. Reservation on Jurisdiction of the International Court," *U.S. Department of State Bulletin,* 42:227 - 232 F 15 '60.

_____, "United Nations, A Cornerstone of U.S. Foreign Policy," *U.S. Depart-ment of State Bulletin,* 41:507 - 508 O 12 '59.

Johnson, L.B. "Direction and Control of Nuclear Power," *U.S. Department of State Bulletin,* 51:458 - 460 O 5 '64

_____, "Russia, China, and England: Our Basic Policy Remains Unchanged." *Vital Speeches,* 31:34 - 36 N 1 '64

_____, and A.J. Goldberg. "World Peace through World Law," *U.S. Depart-ment of State Bulletin,* 53:542 - 548 O 4 '65

Larson, Arthur. "Road Map for the U.N." *Saturday Review,* (April 28, 1962),45:11 - 13 Ap 28 '62.

Lodge, Henry C. " Review of the U.N. Charter," *U.S. Department of State Bulletin,* (March 22, 1954), 30:451 - 452 Mr 22 '54.

_____, "U.N. Emergency Force, Responsibility for All Members," Department of State Bulletin, 41:919 -922 D 21 '59.

MacArthur, Douglass. "Can War be Outlawed from the World?" *U.S. News and World Report,* 38:86 - 88 F 4 '55.

"Memorandum to President Truman: Excerpts from the Federalist Papers," *Saturday Review of Literature,* 31:20 Mr 27 '48.

"Nixon Champions the Rule of Law," *Life,* 46:36 Ap 27 '59.

"Nixon Urges Greater Use of World Court," *Christian Century,* 76:507 Ap 29 '59.

Rusk, Dean. "Building a Recent World Order," *U.S. Department of State Bulletin,* 53:27 - 30 Jl 5 '65.

Stevenson, Adlai E. "A. Stevenson's Last Article: Outline for a New American Policy," *Look,* 29:7 1 - 72 Ag 24 '65.

_____, "American Tradition and Its Implications for International Law, " with bibliography, *U.S. Department of State Bulletin,* 45:959 - 965 D 11 '61.

_____, "Fundamental Meaning of the United Nations: A World of Law and Justice," *Vital Speeches,* 32:615 - 617 Ag 1 '65.

_____, "Past, Present, and Future of the U.N.," *New York Times Magazine,* p. 12, Ja 14 '62.

_____, "United Nations: First Step Toward a World Under Law," U.S. Depart-ment of State Bulletin," 45:68 - 71 Jl 10 '61.

Taft, Robert A. "Law and Justice, The Base of Peace," *Vital Speeches,* 14:15 - 20 O 15 '47.

"Toward a Rule of Law," Senator Humphrey's Resolution. *New Republic,*142:5 - 6 My 9 '60.

Truman, Harry S. "From USA to USW?" President Truman's Call for transformation of the U.N. into a full-fledged world government. *Christian Century,* 63:166 - 168 F 6 '46.

_____, "Truman Message on a United Nations Police Force," *Current History,*39:171 - 174 S '60.

_____, "United Nations. Cornerstone of U.S Foreign Policy," *U.S. Department of State Bulletin,* 27:529 O 6 '52.

Welles, Sumner. "The Atomic Bomb and World Government," *Atlantic,* 177:39 - 42 Ja '46.

Other Prominent Advocates of World Law

Gorbachev, Mikhail. "The River of Time," May 6, 1992 address at Westminster College in Fulton, Missouri. *The Bulletin of the Atomic Scientists,*48:22 - 24 + Jl/Ag '92.

Toynbee, A .J. "Conditions of Survival," *Saturday Review,* 47:24 - 26 + Ag29 '64.

_____, "It is One World or No World," *New York Times Magazine,* p.28, Ap5 '64.

"What We Are For: Summary of New Encyclical on World Peace," by Pope John XXIII," *Time,* 81:60 + Ap 19 '63.

President John F. Kennedy-A Select Bibliography

Chronologically Arranged

Kennedy, John F. "Disarmament," D 11 '59, in Alana Nevins, (ed) *Senator John F. Kennedy: The Strategy of Peace.* New York: Harper and Brothers, 1960.

_____, "A New Twelve Point Agenda in Foreign Policy," *U.S. Congressional Record: Proceedings and Debated of the 86th Congress, Second Session, Vol. 106, Part 10, June 14, 1960.* Washington, D.C.: U.S. Government Printing Office, 1960, pp 12523 - 12526. Point Eleven calls for world peace through the development of world law.

_____, "A Grand and Global Alliance," Excerpt from the Inaugural Address, Ja 20, 1961, in Joseph A. Bagnall, (ed) *President John F. Kennedy's Grand and Global Alliance: World Order for the New Century* Lanham, Maryland: University Press of America, 1992.

_____. "A Truce to Terror," Address before the General Assembly of the United Nations, S 25 '61, *Ibid.,* pp. 27 - 37.

_____, "Establishing the U.S. Arms Control and Disarmament Agency,"Remarks upon Signing the Bill, S 26 '61, *Ibid.,* pp. 39 - 40.

_____, "The Third State of the Union Message," Excerpt. 1 14 '63, *Ibid.,* pp. 45 - 46.

_____, "Disarmament is Our Goal," Address Delivered at Commencement, American University at Washington, D.C., 6 10 '63, *Ibid.,* pp. 47 - 51.

_____, "A Test Ban Treaty is Announced," A Television Address to the People, 7 26 '63, *Ibid.,* pp. 53 - 59.

_____, "Nuclear Test Ban Treaty," Remarks at a News Conference, S 12 '63,*Ibid.,* pp. 61 - 62.

_____, "One World, One Human Race With One Common Destiny," Address before the General Assembly of the United Nations, S 20 '63, *Ibd.*, pp. 61 - 71.

_____, "U.S. Participation in the United Nations, " 17th Annual Report to the Congress of the United States, N 20, '63, *Ibid.*, pp. 79 - 82.

APPENDIX ONE
THE FREEDOM DOCUMENTS

The American Bill of Rights

The American Declaration of Independence

The Universal Declaration of Human Rights

THE AMERICAN BILL OF RIGHTS

Note: The following text is a transcription of the first ten amendments to the Constitution in their original form. These amendments were ratified December 15, 1791, and form what is known as the "Bill of Rights."

Article I

Congress shall make no law respecting an establishment of religion, or prohibiting the free exercise thereof; or abridging the freedom of speech, or of the press; or the right of the people peaceably to assemble, and to petition the Government for a redress of grievances.

Article II

A well regulated Militia, being necessary to the security of a free State, the right of the people to keep and bear Arms, shall not be infringed.

Article III

No Soldier shall, in time of peace be quartered in any house, without the consent of the Owner, nor in time of war, but in a manner to be prescribed by law.

Article IV

The right of the people to be secure in their persons, houses, papers, and effects, against unreasonable searches and seizures, shall not be violated, and no Warrants shall issue, but upon probable cause, supported by Oath or affirmation, and particularly describing the place to be searched, and the persons or things to be seized.

Article V

No person shall be held to answer for a capital, or otherwise infamous crime, unless on a presentment or indictment of a Grand Jury, except in cases arising in the land or naval forces, or in the Militia, when in actual service in time of War or public danger; nor shall any person be subject for the same offence to be twice put in jeopardy of life or limb; nor shall be compelled in any criminal case to be a witness against himself, nor be deprived of life, liberty, or property, without due process of law; nor shall private property be taken for public use, without just compensation.

In all criminal prosecutions, the accused shall enjoy the right to a speedy and public trial, by an impartial jury of the State and district wherein the crime shall have been committed, which district shall have been previously ascertained by law, and to be informed of the nature and cause of the accusation; to be confronted with the witnesses against him; to have compulsory process for obtaining witnesses in his favor, and to have the Assistance of Counsel for his defence.

Article VII

In Suits at common law, where the value in controversy shall exceed twenty dollars, the right of trial by jury shall be preserved, and no fact tried by a jury, shall be otherwise re-examined in any Court of the United States, than according to the rules of the common law.

Article VIII

Excessive bail shall not be required, nor excessive fines imposed, nor cruel and unusual punishments inflicted.

Article IX

The enumeration in the Constitution, of certain rights, shall not be construed to deny or disparage others retained by the people.

Article X

The powers not delegated to the United States by the Constitution, nor prohibited by it to the States, are reserved to the States respectively, or to the people.

The American Declaration of Independence

IN CONGRESS, July 4, 1776.

The Unanimous Declaration
of the Thirteen United States of America,

When in the Course of human events, it becomes necessary for one people to dissolve the political bands which have connected them with another, and to assume among the powers of the earth, the separate and equal station to which the Laws of Nature and of Nature's God entitle them, a decent respect to the opinions of mankind requires that they should declare the causes which impel them to the separation.

We hold these truths to be self-evident, that all men are created equal, that they are endowed by their Creator with certain unalienable Rights, that among these are Life, Liberty and the pursuit of Happiness.--That to secure these rights, Governments are instituted among Men, deriving their just powers from the consent of the governed, --That whenever any Form of Government becomes destructive of these ends, it is the Right of the People to alter or to abolish it, and to institute new Government, laying its foundation on such principles and organizing its powers in such form, as to them shall seem most likely to effect their Safety and Happiness. Prudence, indeed, will dictate that Governments long established should not be changed for light and transient causes; and accordingly all experience hath shown, that mankind are more disposed to suffer, while evils are sufferable, than to right themselves by abolishing the forms to which they are accustomed. But when a long train of abuses and usurpations, pursuing invariably the same Object evinces a design to reduce them under absolute Despotism, it is their right, it is their duty, to throw off such Government, and to provide new Guards for their future security.--Such has been the patient sufferance of these Colonies; and such is now the necessity which constrains them to alter their former Systems of Government. The history of the present King of Great Britain is a history of repeated injuries and usurpations, all having in direct object the establishment of an absolute Tyranny over these States. To prove this, let Facts be submitted to a candid world.

He has refused his Assent to Laws, the most wholesome and necessary for the public good.

He has forbidden his Governors to pass Laws of immediate and pressing importance, unless suspended in their operation till his Assent should be obtained; and when so suspended, he has utterly neglected to attend to them.

He has refused to pass other Laws for the accommodation of large districts of people, unless those people would relinquish the right of Representation in the Legislature, a right inestimable to them and formidable to tyrants only

He has called together legislative bodies at places unusual, uncomfortable, and distant from the depository of their public Records, for the sole purpose of fatiguing them into compliance with his measures.

He has dissolved Representative Houses repeatedly, for opposing with manly firmness his invasions on the rights of the people.

He has refused for a long time, after such dissolutions, to cause others to be elected; whereby the Legislative powers, incapable of Annihilation, have returned to the People at large for their exercise; the State remaining in the mean time exposed to all the dangers of invasion from without, and convulsions within.

He has endeavored to prevent the population of these States; for that purpose obstructing the Laws for Naturalization of Foreigners; refusing to pass others to encourage their migrations hither, and raising the conditions of new Appropriations of Lands.

He has obstructed the Administration of Justice, by refusing his Assent to Laws for establishing Judiciary powers.

He has made Judges dependent on his Will alone, for the tenure of their offices, and the amount and payment of their salaries.

He has erected a multitude of New Offices, and sent hither swarms of Officers to harass our people, and eat out their substance.

He has kept among us, in times of peace, Standing Armies without the Consent of our legislatures.

He has affected to render the Military independent of and superior to the Civil power.

He has combined with others to subject us to a jurisdiction foreign to our constitution, and unacknowledged by our laws; giving his Assent to their Acts of pretended Legislation:

For Quartering large bodies of armed troops among us:
For protecting them, by a mock Trial, from punishment for any Murders which they should commit on the Inhabitants of these States:
For cutting off our Trade with all parts of the world:
For imposing Taxes on us without our Consent:
For depriving us in many cases, of the benefits of Trial by Jury:
For transporting us beyond Seas to be tried for pretended offences
For abolishing the free System of English Laws in a neighboring Province, establishing therein an Arbitrary government, and enlarging its Boundaries so as to render it at once an example and fit instrument for introducing the same absolute rule into these Colonies:
For taking away our Charters, abolishing our most valuable Laws, and altering fundamentally the Forms of our Governments:
For suspending our own Legislatures and declaring themselves invested with power to legislate for us in all cases whatsoever.

He has abdicated Government here, by declaring us out of his Protection and waging War against us.

He has plundered our seas, ravaged our Coasts, burnt our towns, and destroyed the lives of our people.

He is at this time transporting large Armies of foreign Mercenaries to compleat the works of death, desolation and tyranny, already begun with circumstances of Cruelty & perfidy scarcely paralleled in the most barbarous ages, and totally unworthy the Head of a civilized nation.

He has constrained our fellow Citizens taken Captive on the high Seas to bear Arms against their Country, to become the executioners of their friends and Brethren, or to fall themselves by their Hands.
He has excited domestic insurrections amongst us, and has endeavoured to bring on the inhabitants of our frontiers, the merciless Indian Savages, whose known rule of warfare is an undistinguished destruction of all ages, sexes and conditions.

In every stage of these Oppressions We have Petitioned for Redress in the most humble terms: Our repeated Petitions have been answered only by repeated injury. A Prince whose character is thus marked by every act which may define a Tyrant, is unfit to be the ruler of a free people.

Nor have We been wanting in attentions to our British brethren. We have warned them from time to time of attempts by their legislature to extend an unwarrantable jurisdiction over us. We have reminded them of the circumstances of our emigration and settlement here. We have appealed to their native justice and magnanimity, and we have conjured them by the ties of our common kindred to disavow these usurpations, which would inevitably interrupt our connections and correspondence. They too have been deaf to the voice of justice and of consanguinity. We must, necessity, which denounces our Separation, and hold them, as we hold the rest of mankind, Enemies in War, in Peace Friends.

We, therefore, the Representatives of the united States of America, in General Congress, Assembled, appealing to the Supreme Judge of the world for the rectitude of our intentions, do, in the Name, and by Authority of the good People of these Colonies, solemnly publish and declare, That these United Colonies are, and of Right ought to be Free and Independent States; that they are Absolved from all Allegiance to the British Crown, and that all political connection between them and the State of Great Britain, is and ought to be totally dissolved; and that as Free and Independent States, they have full Power to levy War, conclude Peace, contract Alliances, establish Commerce, and to do all other Acts and Things which Independent States may of right do. And for the support of this Declaration, with a firm reliance on the protection of divine Providence, we mutually pledge to each other our Lives, our Fortunes and our sacred Honor.

JOHN HANCOCK [*President*] and fifty-five others

The Universal Declaration of Human Rights

Preamble

Whereas recognition of the inherent dignity and of the equal and inalienable rights of all members of the human family is the foundation of freedom, justice and peace in the world,

Whereas disregard and contempt for human rights have resulted in barbarous acts which have outraged the conscience of mankind, and the advent of a world in which human beings shall enjoy freedom of speech and belief and freedom from fear and want has been proclaimed as the highest aspiration of the common people,

Whereas it is essential, if man is not to be compelled to have recourse, as a last resort, to rebellion against tyranny and oppression, that human rights should be protected by the rule of law,

Whereas it is essential to promote the development of friendly relations between nations,

Whereas the peoples of the United Nations have in the Charter reaffirmed their faith in fundamental human rights, in the dignity and worth of the human person and in the equal rights of men and women and have determined to promote social progress and better standards of life in larger freedom,

Whereas Member States have pledged themselves to achieve, in co-operation with the United Nations, the promotion of Universal respect for and observance of human rights and fundamental freedoms,

Whereas a common understanding of these rights and freedoms is of the greatest importance for the full realization of this pledge,
Now, therefore,

The General Assembly proclaims this

Universal Declaration of Human Rights

Universal Declaration of Human Rights as a common standard of achievement for all peoples and all nations, to the end that every individual and every organ of society, keeping this Declaration constantly in mind, shall strive by teaching and education to promote respect for these rights and freedoms and by progressive measures, national international, to secure their universal and effective recognition and observance, both among the peoples of Member States themselves and among the peoples of territories under their jurisdiction.

Article 1

All human beings are born free and equal in dignity and rights. They are endowed with reason and conscience and should act towards one another in a spirit of brotherhood.

Article 2

Everyone is entitled to all the rights and freedoms set forth in this Declaration, without distinction of any kind, such as race, colour, sex, language, religion, political or other opinion, national or social origin, property, birth or other status. Furthermore, no distinction shall be made on the basis of the political, jurisdictional or international status of the country or territory to which a person belongs, whether it be independent, trust, nonselfgoverning or under any other limitation of sovereignty.

Article 3

Everyone has the right to life, liberty and security of person.

Article 4

No one shall be held in slavery or servitude; slavery and the slave trade shall be prohibited in all their forms.

Article 5

No one shall be subjected to torture or to cruel, inhuman or degrading treatment or punishment.

Article 6

Everyone has the right to recognition everywhere as a person before the law.

Article 7

All are equal before the law and are entitled without any discrimination to equal protection of the law. All are entitled to equal protection against any discrimination in violation of this Declaration and against any incitement to such discrimination.

Article 8

Everyone has the right to an effective remedy by the competent national tribunals for acts violating the fundamental rights granted him by the constitution or by law.

Article 9

No one shall be subjected to arbitrary arrest, detention or exile.

Article 10

Everyone is entitled in full equality to a fair and public hearing by an independent and impartial tribunal, in the determination of his rights and obligations and of any criminal charge against him.

Article 11

1. Everyone charged with a penal offence has the right to be presumed innocent until proved guilty according to law in a public trial at which he has had all the guarantees necessary for his defence.

2. No one shall be held guilty of any penal offence on account of any act or omission which did not constitute a penal offence, under national or international law, at the time when it was committed. Nor shall a heavier penalty be imposed than the one that was applicable at the time the penal offence was committed.

Article 12

No one shall be subjected to arbitrary interference with his privacy, family, home or correspondence, nor to attacks upon his honour and reputation.

Everyone has the right to the protection of the law against such interference or attacks.

Article 13

1. Everyone has the right to freedom of movement and residence within the borders of each state.

2. Everyone has the right to leave any country, including his own, and to return to his country.

Article 14

1. Everyone has the right to seek and to enjoy in other countries asylum from persecution.

2. This right may not be invoked in the case of prosecutions genuinely arising from non-political crimes or from acts contrary to the purposes and principles of the United Nations.

Article 15

1. Everyone has the right to a nationality.

2. No one shall be arbitrarily deprived of his nationality nor denied the right to change his nationality.

Article 16

1. Men and women of full age, without any limitation due to race, nationality or religion, have the right to marry and to found a family. They are entitled to equal rights as to marriage, during marriage and at its dissolution.

2. Marriage shall be entered into only with the free and full consent of the intending spouses.

3. The family is the natural and fundamental group unit of society and is entitled to protection by society and the State.

Article 17

1. Everyone has the right to own property alone as well as in association with others.

2. No one shall be arbitrarily deprived of his property.

Article 18

Everyone has the right to freedom of thought, conscience and religion; this right includes freedom to change his religion or belief, and freedom, either alone or in community with others and in public or private, to manifest his religion or belief in teaching, practice, worship and observance.

Article 19

Everyone has the right to freedom of opinion and expression; this right includes freedom to hold opinions without interference and to seek, receive and impart information and ideas through any media and regardless of frontiers.

Article 20

1. Everyone has the right to freedom of peaceful assembly and association.

2. No one may be compelled to belong to an association.

Article 21

1. Everyone has the right to take part in the government of his country, directly or through freely chosen representatives.

2. Everyone has the right of equal access to public service in his country.

3. The will of the people shall be the basis of the authority of government; this will shall be expressed in periodic and genuine elections which shall be by universal and equal suffrage and shall be held by secret vote or by equivalent free voting procedures.

Article 22

Everyone, as a member of society, has the right to a social security and is entitled to realization, through national effort and international co-operation and in accordance with the organization and resources of each State, of the economic, social and cultural rights indispensable for his dignity and the free development of his personality.

Article 23

1. Everyone has the right to work, to free choice of employment, to just and favourable conditions of work and to protection against unemployment.

2. Everyone, without any discrimination, has the right to equal pay for equal work.

3. Everyone who works has the right to just and favourable remuneration ensuring for himself and his family an existence worthy of human dignity, and supplemented, if necessary, by other means of social protection.

4. Everyone has the right to form and to join trade unions for the protection of his interests.

Article 24

Everyone has the right to rest and leisure, including reasonable limitation of working hours and periodic holidays with pay.

Article 25

1. Everyone has the right to a standard of living adequate for the health and well-being of himself and of his family, including food, clothing, housing and medical care and necessary social services, and the right to security in the event of unemployment, sickness, disability, widowhood, old age or other lack of livelihood in circumstances beyond his control.

2. Motherhood and childhood are entitled to special care and assistance. All children, whether born in or out of wedlock, shall enjoy the same social protection.

Article 26

1. Everyone has the right to education. Education shall be free, at least in the elementary and fundamental stages. Elementary education shall be compulsory. Technical and professional education shall be made generally available and higher education shall be equally accessible to all on the basis of merit.

2. Education shall be directed to the full development of the human personality and to the strengthening of respect for human rights and fundamental freedoms. It shall promote understanding, tolerance and friendship among all nations, racial or religious groups, and shall further the activities of the United Nations for the maintenance of peace.

3. Parents have a prior right to choose the kind of education that shall be given to their children.

Article 27

1. Everyone has the right freely to participate in the cultural life of the community, to enjoy the arts and to share in scientific advancement and its benefits.

2. Everyone has the right to the protection of the moral and material interests resulting from any scientific, literary or artistic production of which he is the author.

Article 28

Everyone is entitled to a social and international order in which the rights and freedoms set forth in this Declaration can be fully realized.

Article 29

1. Everyone has duties to the community in which alone the free and full development of his personality is possible.

2. In the exercise of his rights and freedoms, everyone shall be subject only to such limitations as are determined by law solely for the purpose of securing due recognition and respect for the rights and freedoms of others and of meeting the just requirements of morality, public order and the general welfare in a democratic society.

3. These rights and freedoms may in no case be exercised contrary to the purposes and principles of the United Nations.

Article 30

Nothing in this Declaration may be interpreted as implying for any State, group or person any right to engage in any activity or to perform any act aimed at the destruction of any of the rights and freedoms set forth herein.

Appendix Two

The Charter of the United Nations
and the Statute of
the International Court of Justice

The Charter of the United Nations
And the Statute of
The International Court of Justice

We the peoples of the United Nations determined

to save succeeding generations from the scourge of war which twice in our lifetime has brought untold sorrow to mankind, and

to reaffirm faith in fundamental human rights, in the dignity and worth of the human person, in the equal rights of men and women and of nations large and small, and

to establish conditions under which justice and respect for the obligations arising from treaties and other sources of international law can be maintained, and

to promote social progress and better standards of life in larger freedom.

and for these ends

to practice tolerance and live together in peace with one another as good neighbors, and

to unite our strength to maintain international peace and security, and

to ensure, by the acceptance of principles and the institution of methods, that armed force shall not be used, save in the common interest, and

to employ international machinery for the promotion of the economic and social advancement of all peoples

have resolved to combine our efforts to accomplish these aims.

Accordingly, our respective Governments, through representatives assembled in the city of San Francisco, who have exhibited their

full powers found to be in good and due form, have agreed to the present Charter of the United Nations and do hereby establish an international organization to be known as the United Nations.

Chapter I
PURPOSES AND PRINCIPLES

Article 1

The Purposes of the United Nations are:

1. To maintain international peace and security, and to that end: to take effective collective measures for the prevention and removal of threats to the peace, and for the suppression of acts of aggression or other breaches of the peace, and to bring about by peaceful means, and in conformity with the principles of justice and international law, adjustment or settlement of international disputes or situations which might lead to a breach of the peace.

2. To develop friendly relations among nations based on respect for the principle of equal rights and self-determination of peoples, and to take other appropriate measures to strengthen universal peace;

3. To achieve international cooperation in solving international problems of an economic, social, cultural, or humanitarian character, and in promoting and encouraging respect for human rights and for fundamental freedoms for all without distinction as to race, sex, language, or religion; and

4. To be a center for harmonizing the actions of nations in the attainment of these common ends.

Article 2

The organization and its Members, in pursuit of the Purposes stated in Article 1, shall act in accordance with the following Principles.

1. The Organization is based on the principle of the sovereign equality of all its Members.

2. All Members, in order to ensure to all of them the rights and benefits resulting from membership, shall fulfill in good faith the obligations assumed by them in accordance with the present Charter.

3. All Members shall settle their international disputes by peaceful means in such a manner that international peace and security, and justice, are not endangered.

4. All Members shall refrain in their international relations from the threat or use of force against the territorial integrity or political independence of any state, or in any other manner inconsistent with the Purposes of the United Nations.

5. All Members shall give the United Nations every assistance in any action it takes in accordance with the present Charter, and shall refrain from giving assistance to any state against which the United Nations is taking preventative or enforcement action.

6. The Organization shall ensure that states which are not Members of the United Nations act in accordance with these Principles so far as may be necessary for the maintenance of international peace and security.

7. Nothing contained in the present Charter shall authorize the United Nations to intervene in matters which are essentially within the domestic jurisdiction of any state or shall require the Members to submit such matters to settlement under the present Charter; but this principle shall not prejudice the application of enforcement measures under Chapter VII.

Chapter II
MEMBERSHIP

Article 3

The original Members of the United Nations shall be the states which, having participated in the United Nations Conference on International Organization at San Francisco, or having previously signed the Declaration by United Nations of January 1, 1942, sign the present Charter and ratify it in accordance with Article 110.

Article 4

1. Membership in the United Nations is open to all other peace-loving states which accept the obligations contained in the present Charter and, in the judgment of the Organization, are able and willing to carry out these obligations.

2. The admission of any such state to membership in the United Nations will be effected by a decision of the General Assembly upon the recommendation of the Security Council.

Article 5

A Member of the United Nations against which preventive or enforcement action has been taken by the Security Council may be suspended from the exercise of the rights and privileges of membership by the General Assembly upon the recommendation of the Security Council. The exercise of these rights and privileges may be restored by the Security Council.

Article 6

A Member of the United Nations which has persistently violated the Principles contained in the present Charter may be expelled from the Organization by the General Assembly upon the recommendation of the Security Council.

Chapter III
ORGANS

Article 7

1. There are established as the principal organs of the United Nations: A General Assembly, a Security Council, an Economic and Social Council, a Trusteeship Council, an International Court of Justice, and a Secretariat.

2. Such subsidiary organs as may be found necessary may be established in accordance with the present Charter.

Article 8

The United Nations shall place no restrictions on the eligibility of men and women to participate in any capacity and under conditions of equality in its principal and subsidiary organs.

Chapter IV
THE GENERAL ASSEMBLY

COMPOSITION

Article 9

1. The General Assembly shall consist of all Members of the United Nations.

2. Each Member shall have not more than five representatives in the General Assembly.

FUNCTIONS AND POWERS

Article 10

The General Assembly may discuss any questions or any matters within the scope of the present Charter or relating to the powers and functions of any organs provided for in the present Charter, and except as provided in Article 12, may make recommendations to the Members of the United Nations or to the Security Council or to both on any such questions or matters.

Article 11

1. The General Assembly may consider the general principles of cooperation in the maintenance of international peace and security, including the principles governing disarmament and the regulation of armaments, and may make recommendations with regard to such principles to the Members or to the Security Council or to both.

2. The General Assembly may discuss any questions relating to the maintenance of international peace and security brought before it by any Member of the United Nations, or by the Security Council, or by a state which is not a Member of the United Nations in accordance with Article 35, paragraph 2, and except as provided in Article 12, may make recommendations with regard to any such questions to the state or states concerned or to the Security Council or to both. Any such question on which action is necessary shall be referred to the Security Council by the General Assembly either before or after discussion.

3. The General Assembly may call the attention of the Security Council to situations which are likely to endanger international peace and security.

4. The powers of the General Assembly set forth in this Article shall not limit the general scope of Article 10.

Article 12

1. While the Security Council is exercising in respect of any dispute or situation the functions assigned to it in the present Charter, the General Assembly shall not make any recommendation with regard to that dispute or situation unless the Security Council so requests.

2. The Secretary-General, with the consent of the Security Council, shall notify the General Assembly at each session of any matters relative to the maintenance of international peace and security which are being dealt with by the Security Council and shall similarly notify the General Assembly, or the Members of the United Nations if the General Assembly is not in session, immediately the Security Council ceases to deal with such matters.

Article 13

1. The General Assembly shall initiate studies and make recommendations for the purpose of:

a.   promoting international cooperation in the political field and encouraging the progressive development of international law and its codification;

b.   promoting international cooperation in the economic, social, cultural, educational, and health fields, and assisting in the realization of human rights and fundamental freedoms for all without distinction as to race, sex, language, or religion.

2.   The further responsibilities, functions, and powers of the General Assembly with respect to matters mentioned in paragraph 1 (b) above are set forth in Chapters IX and X.

Article 14

Subject to the provisions of Article 12, the General Assembly may recommend measures for the peaceful adjustment of any situation, regardless of origin, which it deems likely to impair the general welfare or friendly relations among nations, including situations resulting from a violation of the provisions of the present Charter setting forth the Purposes and Principles of the United Nations.

Article 15

1.   The General Assembly shall receive and consider annual and special reports from the Security Council; these reports shall include an account of the measures that the Security Council has decided upon or taken to maintain international peace and security.

2.   The General Assembly shall receive and consider reports from the other organs of the United Nations.

Article 16

The General Assembly shall perform such functions with respect to the international trusteeship system as are assigned to it under Chapters XII and XIII, including the approval of the trusteeship agreements for areas not designated as strategic.

Article 17

1. The General Assembly shall consider and approve the budget of the Organization.

2. The expenses of the Organization shall be borne by the Members as apportioned by the General Assembly.

3. The General Assembly shall consider and approve any financial and budgetary arrangements with specialized agencies referred to in Article 57 and shall examine the administrative budgets of such specialized agencies with a view to making recommendations to the agencies concerned.

VOTING

Article 18

1. Each member of the General Assembly shall have one vote.

2. Decisions of the General Assembly on important questions hall be made by a two-thirds majority of the members present and voting. These questions shall include: recommendations with respect to the maintenance of international peace and security, the election of the non-permanent members of the Security Council, the election of the members of the Economic and social Council, the election of members of the Trusteeship Council in accordance with paragraph 1 (c) of Article 86, the admission of new Members to the United Nations, the suspension of the rights and privileges of membership, the expulsion of Members, questions relating to the operation of the trusteeship system, and budgetary questions.

3. Decisions on other questions, including the determination of additional categories of questions to be decided by a two-thirds majority, shall be made by a majority of the members present and voting.

Article 19

A Member of the United Nations which is in arrears in the payment of its financial contributions to the Organization shall have no vote in the General Assembly if the amount of its arrears equals or exceeds the amount of the contributions due from it for the preceding two full years. The General Assembly may, nevertheless, permit such a Member to vote if it is satisfied that the failure to pay is due to conditions beyond the control of the Member.

PROCEDURE

Article 20

The General Assembly shall meet in regular annual sessions and in such special sessions as occasion may require. Special sessions shall be convoked by the Secretary-General at the request of the Security Council or of a majority of the Members of the United Nations.

PROCEDURE

Article 21

The General Assembly shall adopt its own rules of procedure. It shall elect its President for each session.

Article 22

The General Assembly may establish such subsidiary organs as it deems necessary for the performance of its functions.

Chapter V
THE SECURITY COUNCIL

COMPOSITION

Article 23 (as amended in 1965)

1. The Security Council shall consist of fifteen members of the United Nations. The Republic of China, France, the Union of Soviet Socialist Republics, the United Kingdom of Great Britain and Northern Ireland, and the United States of America shall be permanent members of the Security Council. The General Assembly shall elect ten other Members of the United Nations to

be non-permanent members of the Security Council, due regard being specially paid, in the first instance to the contribution of Members of the United Nations to the maintenance of international peace and security and to the other purposes of the Organization, and also to equitable geographical distribution.

2. The non-permanent members of the Security Council shall be elected for a term of two years. In the first election of the non-permanent members after the increase of the membership of the Security Council from eleven to fifteen, two of the four additional members shall be chosen for a term of one year. A retiring member shall not be eligible for immediate re-election.

3. Each member of the Security Council shall have one representative.

FUNCTIONS AND POWERS

Article 24

1. In order to ensure prompt and effective action by the United Nations, its Members confer on the Security Council primary responsibility for the maintenance of international peace and security, and agree that in carrying out its duties under this responsibility the Security Council acts on their behalf.

2. In discharging these duties the Security Council shall act in accordance with the Purposes and Principles of the United Nations. The specific powers granted to the Security Council for the discharge of these duties are laid down in Chapters VI, VII, VIII, and XII.

3. The Security Council shall submit annual and, when necessary, special reports to the General Assembly for its consideration.

Article 25

The Members of the United Nations agree to accept and carry out the decisions of the Security Council in accordance with the present Charter.

Article 26

In order to promote the establishment and maintenance of international peace and security with the least diversion for armaments of the world's human and economic resources, the Security Council shall be responsible for formulating, with the assistance of the Military Staff Committee referred to in Article 47, plans to be submitted to the Members of the United Nations for the establishment of a system for the regulation of armaments.

VOTING

Article 27 (as amended in 1965)

1. Each member of the Security Council shall have one vote.

2. Decisions of the Security Council on procedural matters shall be made by an affirmative vote of nine members.

3. Decisions of the Security Council on all other matters shall be made by an affirmative vote of nine members including the concurring votes of the permanent members; provided that, in decisions under Chapter VI and under paragraph 3 of Article 52, a party to a dispute shall abstain from voting.

PROCEDURE

Article 28

1. The Security Council shall be so organized as to be able to function continuously. Each member of the Security Council shall for this purpose be represented at all times at the seat of the Organization.

2. The Security Council shall hold periodic meetings at which each of its members may, if it so desires, be represented by a member of the government or by some other specially designated representative.

3. The Security Council may hold meetings at such places other than the seat of the Organization as in its judgment will best facilitate its work.

Article 29

The Security Council may establish such subsidiary organs as it deems necessary for the performance of its functions.

Article 30

The Security Council shall adopt its own rules of procedure, including the method of selecting its President.

Article 31

Any member of the United Nations which is not a member of the Security Council may participate, without vote, in the discussion of any question brought before the Security Council whenever the latter considers that the interests of that Member are specially affected.

Article 32

Any Member of the United Nations which is not a member of the Security Council or any state which is not a Member of the United Nations, if it is a party to a dispute under consideration by the Security Council, shall be invited to participate, without vote, in the discussion relating to the dispute. The Security Council shall lay down such conditions as it deems just for the participation of a state which is not a Member of the United Nations.

Chapter VI
PACIFIC SETTLEMENT OF DISPUTES

Article 33

1. The Parties to any dispute, the continuance of which is likely to endanger the maintenance of international peace and security, shall, first of all, seek a solution by negotiation, enquiry, mediation, conciliation, arbitration, judicial settlement, resort to regional agencies or arrangements, or other peaceful means of their own choice.

2. The Security Council shall, when it deems necessary, call upon the parties to settle their dispute by such means.

Article 34

The Security Council may investigate any dispute, or any situation which might lead to international friction or give arise to a dispute, in order to determine whether the continuance of the dispute or situation is likely to endanger the maintenance of international peace and security.

Article 35

1. Any Member of the United Nations may bring any dispute, or any situation of the nature referred to in Article 34, to the attention of the Security Council or of the General Assembly.

2. A state which is not a Member of the United Nations may bring to the attention of the Security Council or of the General Assembly any dispute to which it is a party if it accepts in advance, for the purposes of the dispute, the obligations of pacific settlement provided in the present Charter.

3. The proceedings of the General Assembly in respect of matters brought to its attention under this Article will be subject to the provisions of Articles 11 and 12.

Article 36

1. The Security Council may, at any stage of a dispute of the nature referred to in Article 33 or of a situation of like nature, recommend appropriate procedures or methods of adjustment.

2. The Security Council should take into consideration any procedures for the settlement of the dispute which have already been adopted by the parties.

3. In making recommendations under this Article the Security Council should also take into consideration that legal disputes should as a general rule be referred by the parties to the International Court of Justice in accordance with the provisions of the Statute of the Court.

Article 37

1. Should the parties to a dispute of the nature referred to in Article 33 fail to settle it by the means indicated in that Article, they shall refer it to the Security Council.

2. If the Security Council deems that the continuance of the dispute is in fact likely to endanger the maintenance of international peace and security, it shall decide whether to take action under Article 36 or to recommend such terms of settlement as it may consider appropriate.

Article 38

Without prejudice to the provisions of Article 33 to 37, the Security Council may, if all the parties to any dispute so request, make recommendations to the parties with a view to a pacific settlement of the dispute.

Chapter VII
ACTION WITH RESPECT TO THREATS TO THE PEACE, BREACHES OF THE PEACE, AND ACTS OF AGGRESSION

Article 39

The Security Council shall determine the existence of any threat to the peace, breach of the peace, or act of aggression and shall make recommendations, or decide what measures shall be taken in accordance with Articles 41 and 42, to maintain or restore international peace and security.

Article 40

In order to prevent an aggravation of the situation, the Security council may, before making the recommendations or deciding upon the measures provided for in Article 39, call upon the parties concerned to comply with such provisional measures as it deems necessary or desirable. Such provisional measures shall be without prejudice to the rights, claims, or position of the parties concerned. The Security Council shall duly take account of failure to comply with such provisional measures.

Article 41

The Security Council may decide what measure not involving the use of armed force are to be employed to give effect to its decisions, and it may call upon the Members of the United Nations to apply such measures. These may include complete or partial interruption of economic relations and of rail, sea, air, postal, telegraphic, radio, and other means of communication, and the severance of diplomatic relations.

Article 42

Should the Security Council consider that measures provided for in Article 41 would be inadequate or have proved to be inadequate, it may take such action by air, sea, or land forces as may be necessary to maintain or restore international peace and security. Such action may include demonstrations, blockade, and other operations by air, sea, or land forces of Members of the United Nations.

Article 43

1. All Members of the United Nations, in order to contribute to the maintenance of international peace and security, undertake to make available to the Security Council, on its call and in accordance with a special agreement or agreements, armed forces, assistance, and facilities including rites of passage, necessary for the purpose of maintaining international peace and security.

2. Such agreement or agreements shall govern the numbers and types of forces, their degree of readiness and general location, and the nature of the facilities and assistance to be provided.

3. The agreement or agreements shall be negotiated as soon as possible on the initiative of the Security Council. They shall be concluded between the Security Council and Members or between the Security Council and groups of Members and shall be subject to ratification by the signatory states in accordance with their respective constitutional processes.

Article 44

When the Security Council has decided to use force it shall, before calling upon a Member not represented on it to provide armed forces in fulfillment of the obligations assumed under Article 43, invite that Member, if the Member so desires, to participate in the decisions of the Security Council concerning the employment of contingents of that Member's armed forces.

Article 45

In order to enable the United Nations to take urgent military measure, Members shall hold immediately available national air-force contingents for combined international enforcement action. The strength and degree of readiness of these contingents and plans for their combined action shall be determined, within the limits laid down in the special agreement or agreements referred to inn Article 43, by the Security Council with the assistance of the Military Staff Committee.

Article 46

Plans for the application of armed force shall be made by the Security Council with the assistance of the Military Staff Committee.

Article 47

1. There shall be established a Military Staff Committee to advise and assist the Security Council on all questions relating to the Security Council's military requirements for the maintenance of international peace and security, the employment and command of forces placed at its disposal, the regulation of armaments, and possible disarmament.

2. The Military Staff Committee shall consist of the Chiefs of Staff of the permanent members of the Security Council or their representatives. Any Member of the United Nations not permanently represented on the Committee shall be invited by the Committee to be associated with it when the efficient discharge of the Committee's responsibilities requires the participation of that Member in its work.

3. The Military Staff Committee shall be responsible under the Security Council for the strategic direction of any armed forces placed at the disposal of the Security Council. Questions

relating to the command of such forces shall be worked out subsequently.

4. The Military Staff Committee, with the authorization of the Security Council and after consultation, with appropriate regional agencies, may establish regional sub-committees.

Article 48

1. The action required to carry out the decisions of the Security Council for the maintenance of international peace and security shall be taken by all the Members of the United Nations or by some of them, as the Security council may determine.

2. Such decisions shall be carried out by the Members of the United Nations directly and through their action in the appropriate international agencies of which they are members.

Article 49

The Members of the United Nations shall join in affording mutual assistance in carrying out the measures decided upon by the Security Council.

Article 50

If preventive or enforcement measures against any state are taken by the Security council, any other state, whether a Member of the United Nations or not, which finds itself confronted with special economic problems arising from the carrying out of those measures shall have the right to consult the Security Council with regard to a solution of those problems.

Article 51

Nothing in the present Charter shall impair the inherent right of individual or collective self-defense if an armed attack occurs against a Member of the United Nations, until the Security Council has taken the measures necessary to maintain international peace and security. Measures taken by Members in the exercise of this right of self-defense shall be immediately reported to the Security Council and shall not in any way affect the authority and responsibility of the Security Council under the present Charter to take at any time such action as it deems necessary in order to maintain or restore international peace and security.

Chapter VIII
REGIONAL ARRANGEMENTS

Article 52

1. Nothing in the present Charter precludes the existence of regional arrangements or agencies for dealing with such matters relating to the maintenance of international peace and security as are appropriate for regional action, provided that such arrangements or agencies and their activities are consistent with the Purposes and Principles of the United Nations.

2. The Members of the United Nations entering into such arrangements or constituting such agencies shall make every effort to achieve pacific settlement of local disputes through such regional arrangements or by such regional agencies before referring them to the Security Council.

3. The Security Council shall encourage the development of pacific settlement of local disputes through such regional arrangements or by such regional agencies either on the initiative of the states concerned or by reference from the Security Council.

4. This Article in no way impairs the application of Articles 34 and 35.

Article 53

1. The Security Council shall, where appropriate, utilize such regional arrangements or agencies for enforcement action under its authority. But no enforcement action shall be taken under regional arrangements or by regional agencies without the authorization of the Security Council with the exception of measures against any enemy state, as defined in paragraph 2 of this Article, provided for pursuant to Article 107 or in regional arrangements directed against renewal of aggressive policy on the part of any such state, until such time as the Organization may,

on request of the Governments concerned, be charged with the responsibility for preventing further aggression by such a state.

2. The term enemy state as used in paragraph 1 of this Article applies to any state which during the Second World War has been an enemy of any signatory of the present Charter.

Article 54

The Security Council shall at all times be kept fully informed of activities undertaken or in contemplation under regional arrangements or by regional agencies for the maintenance of international peace and security.

Chapter IX
INTERNATIONAL ECONOMIC AND SOCIAL COOPERATION

Article 55

With a view to the creation of conditions of stability and well-being which are necessary for peaceful and friendly relations among nations based on respect for the principle of equal rights and self-determination of peoples, the United nations shall promote:

a. higher standards of living, full employment, and conditions of economic and social progress and development;

b. solutions of international economic, social, health, and related problems; and international cultural and educational cooperation; and

c. universal respect for, and observance of, human rights and fundamental freedoms for all without distinction as to race, sex, language, or religion.

Article 56

All Members pledge themselves to take joint and separate action in cooperation with the Organization for the achievement of the purposes set forth in Article 55.

Article 57

1. The various specialized agencies, established by intergovernmental agreement and having wide international responsibilities, as defined in their basic instruments, in economic, social, cultural, educational, health, and related fields, shall be brought into relationship with the United Nations in accordance with the provisions of Article 63.

2. Such agencies thus brought into relationship with the United Nations are hereinafter referred to as specialized agencies.

Article 58

The Organization shall make recommendations for the coordination of the policies and activities of the specialized agencies.

Article 59

The Organization shall, where appropriate, initiate negotiations among the states concerned for the creation of any new specialized agencies required for the accomplishment of the purposes set forth in Article 55.

Article 60

Responsibility for the discharge of the functions of the Organization set forth in this Chapter shall be vested in the General Assembly and, under the authority of the General Assembly, in the Economic and Social Council, which shall have for this purpose the powers set forth in Chapter X.

Chapter X
THE ECONOMIC AND SOCIAL COUNCIL

COMPOSITION

Article 61 (as amended in 1973)

1. The Economic and Social Council shall consist of fifty-four Members of the United Nations elected by the General Assembly.

2. Subject to the provisions of paragraph 3, eighteen members of the Economic and Social Council shall be elected each year for a term of three years. A retiring member shall be eligible for immediate re-election.

3. At the first election after the increase in the membership of the Economic and Social Council from twenty-seven to fifty-four members, in addition to the members elected in place of the nine members whose term of office expires at the end of that year, twenty-seven additional members shall be elected. Of these twenty-seven additional members, the term of office of nine members so elected shall expire at the end of one year, and of nine other members at the end of two years, in accordance with arrangements made by the General Assembly.

4. Each member of the Economic and Social Council shall have one representative.

FUNCTIONS AND POWERS

Article 62

1. The Economic and Social council may make or initiate studies and reports with respect to international economic, social, cultural, educational, health, and related matters and may make recommendations with respect to any such matters to the General Assembly, to the Members of the United Nations, and to the specialized agencies concerned.

2. It may make recommendations for the purpose of promoting respect for, and observance of, human rights and fundamental freedoms for all.

3. It may prepare draft conventions for submission to the General Assembly, with respect to matters falling within its competence.

4. It may call, in accordance with the rules prescribed by the United Nations, international conferences on matters falling within its competence.

Article 63

1. The Economic and Social Council may enter into agreements with any of the agencies referred to in Article 57, defining the terms on which the agency concerned shall be brought into relationship with the United Nations. Such agreements shall be subject to approval by the General Assembly.

2. It may coordinate the activities of the specialized agencies through consultation with and recommendations to such agencies and through recommendations to the General Assembly and to the Members of the United Nations.

Article 64

1. The Economic and Social Council may take appropriate steps to obtain regular reports from the specialized agencies. It may make arrangements with the Members of the United Nations and with the specialized agencies to obtain reports on the steps taken to give effect to its own recommendations to recommendations on matters falling within its competence made by the General Assembly.

2. It may communicate its observations on these reports to the General Assembly.

Article 65

The Economic and Social Council may furnish information to the Security Council and shall assist the Security Council upon its request.

Article 66

1. The Economic and Social Council shall perform such functions as fall within its competence in connection with the carrying out of the recommendations of the General Assembly.

2. It may, with the approval of the General Assembly, perform services at the request of Members of the United Nations and at the request of specialized agencies.

3. It shall perform such other functions as are specified elsewhere in the present Charter or as may be assigned to it by the General Assembly.

VOTING

Article 67

1. Each member of the Economic and Social Council shall have one vote.

2. Decisions of the Economic and Social Council shall be made by a majority of the members present and voting.

PROCEDURE

Article 68

The Economic and Social Council shall set up commissions in economic and social fields and for the promotion of human rights, and such other commissions as may be required for the performance of its functions.

Article 69

The Economic and Social Council shall invite any Member of the United Nations to participate, without vote, in its deliberations on any matter of particular concern to that Member.

Article 70

The Economic and Social Council may make arrangements for representatives of the specialized agencies to participate, without vote, in its deliberations and in those of the commissions established by it, and for its representatives to participate in the deliberations of the specialized agencies.

Article 71

The Economic and Social Council may make suitable arrangements for consultation with non-governmental organizations which are concerned with matters within its competence. Such arrangements may be made with international organizations and, where appropriate, with national organizations after consultation with the Member of the United Nations concerned.

Article 72

1. The Economic and Social Council shall adopt its own rules of procedure, including the method of selecting its President.

2. The Economic and Social Council shall meet as required in accordance with its rules, which shall include provision for the convening of meetings on the request of a majority of its members.

Chapter XI
DECLARATION REGARDING NON-SELF-GOVERNING TERRITORIES

Article 73

Members of the United Nations which have or assume responsibilities for the administration of territories whose people have not yet attained a full measure of self-government recognize the principle that the interests of the inhabitants of these territories are paramount, and accept as a sacred trust, the obligation to promote to the utmost, within the system of international peace and security established by the present Charter, the well-being of the inhabitants of these territories, and, to this end:

a. to ensure, with due respect for the culture of the people concerned, their political, economic, social, and educational advancement, their just treatment, and their protection against abuses;

b. to develop self-government, to take due account of the political aspirations of the people, and to assist them in the progressive development of their free political institutions, according to the particular circumstances of each territory and its peoples and their varying stages of advancement;

c. to further international peace and security;

d. to promote constructive measures of development, to encourage research, and to cooperate with one another and, when and where appropriate, with specialized international bodies with a view to the practical achievement of the social, economic, and scientific purposes set forth in this Article; and

e.   to transmit regularly to the Secretary-General for information purposes, subject to such limitation as security and constitutional considerations may require, statistical and other information of a technical nature relating to economic, social, and educational conditions in the territories for which they are respectively responsible other than those territories to which Chapters XII and XIII apply.

Article 74

Members of the United Nations also agree that their policy in respect of the territories to which this Chapter applies, no less than in respect of their metropolitan areas, must be based on the general principle of good-neighborliness, due account being taken of the interests and well-being of the rest of the world, in social economic, and commercial matters.

Chapter XII
INTERNATIONAL TRUSTEESHIP SYSTEM

Article 75

The United Nations shall establish under its authority an international trusteeship system for the administration and supervision of such territories as may be placed thereunder by subsequent individual agreements. Those territories are hereinafter referred to as trust territories.

Article 76

The basic objectives of the trusteeship system, in accordance with the Purposes of the United Nations laid down in Article 1 of the present Charter, shall be:

a.   to further international peace and security;

b.   to promote the political, economic, social, and educational advancement of the inhabitants of the trust territories, and their progressive development towards self-government or independence as may be appropriate to the particular circumstances of each territory and its peoples and the freely expressed wishes of the peoples concerned and as may be provided by the terms of each trusteeship agreement;

c.   to encourage respect for human rights and for fundamental freedoms for all without distinction as to race, sex, language, or religion, and to encourage recognition of the interdependence of the peoples of the world; and

d.   to ensure equal treatment in social, economic, and commercial matters for all Members of the United Nations and their nationals, and also equal treatment for the latter in the administration of justice, without prejudice to the attainment of the foregoing objectives and subject to the provisions of Article 80.

Article 77

1.   The trusteeship system shall apply to such territories in the following categories as may be placed thereunder by means of trusteeship agreements:

    a.   territories now held under mandate;

    b.   territories which may be detached from enemy states as a result of the Second World War; and

    c.   territories voluntarily placed under the system by states responsible for their administration.

2.   It will be a matter for subsequent agreement as to which territories in the foregoing categories will be brought under the trusteeship system and upon what terms.

Article 78

The trusteeship system shall not apply to territories which have become Members of the United Nations, relationship among which shall be based on respect for the principle of sovereign equality.

Article 79

The terms of trusteeship for each territory to be placed under the trusteeship system, including any alteration or amendment, shall be agreed upon by the states directly concerned, including the mandatory power in the case of territories held under mandate by a Member of the United Nations, and shall be approved as provided for in Articles 83 and 85.

Article 80

1. Except as may be agreed upon in individual trusteeship agreements, made under Articles 77, 79, and 81, placing each territory under the trusteeship system, and until such agreements have been concluded, nothing in this Chapter shall be construed in or of itself to alter in any manner the rights whatsoever of any states or any peoples or the terms of existing international instruments to which Members of the United Nations may respectively be parties.

2. Paragraph 1 of this Article shall not be interpreted as giving ground for delay or postponement of the negotiation and conclusion of agreements for placing mandated and other territories under the trusteeship system as provided for in Article 77.

Article 81

The trusteeship agreement shall in each case include the terms under which the trust territory will be administered and designate the authority which will exercise the administration of the trust territory. Such authority may be one or more states or the Organization itself.

Article 82

There may be designated, in any trusteeship agreement, a strategic area or areas which may include part or all of the trust territory to which the agreement applies, without prejudice to any special agreement or agreements made under Article 43.

Article 83

1. All functions of the United Nations relating to strategic areas, including the approval of the terms of the trusteeship agreements and of their alteration or amendment, shall be exercised by the Security Council.

2. The basic objectives set forth in Article 76 shall be applicable to the people of each strategic area.

3. The Security Council shall, subject to the provisions of the trusteeship agreements and without prejudice to security considerations, avail itself of the assistance of the Trusteeship Council to perform those functions of the United Nations under the trusteeship system relating to political, economic, social, and educational matters in the strategic areas.

Article 84

It shall be the duty of the administering authority to ensure that the trust territory shall play its part in the maintenance of international peace and security. To this end the administering authority may make use of volunteer forces, facilities, and assistance from the trust territory in carrying out the obligations towards the Security Council undertaken in this regard by the administering authority, as well as for local defense and the maintenance of law and order within the trust territory.

Article 85

1. The functions of the United Nations with regard to trusteeship agreements for all areas not designated as strategic, including the approval of the terms of the trusteeship agreements and of their alteration or amendment, shall be exercised by the General Assembly.

2. The Trusteeship Council, operating under the authority of the General Assembly, shall assist the General Assembly in carrying out these functions.

Chapter XIII
THE TRUSTEESHIP COUNCIL

COMPOSITION

Article 86

1. The Trusteeship Council shall consist of the following Members of the United Nations:

a. those Members administering trust territories;

b. such of those Members mentioned by name in Article 23 as are not administering trust territories; and

c. as many other Members elected for three-year terms by the General Assembly as may be necessary to ensure that the total number of members of the Trusteeship Council is equally divided between those Members of the United Nations which administer trust territories and those which do not.

2. Each member of the Trusteeship Council shall designate one specially qualified person to represent it therein.

FUNCTIONS AND POWERS

Article 87

The General Assembly and, under its authority, the Trusteeship Council, in carry out their functions, may:

a. consider reports submitted by the administering authority;

b. accept petitions and examine them in consultation with the administering authority;

c. provide for periodic visits to the respective trust territories at times agreed upon with the administering authority; and

d. take these and other actions in conformity with the terms of the trusteeship agreements.

Article 88

The Trusteeship Council shall formulate a questionnaire on the political, economic, social, and educational advancement of the inhabitants of each trust territory, and the administering authority for each trust territory within the competence of the General Assembly shall make an annual report to the General Assembly upon the basis of such questionnaire.

VOTING

Article 89

1. Each member of the Trusteeship Council shall have one vote.

2. Decisions of the Trusteeship Council shall be made by a majority of the members present and voting.

PROCEDURE

Article 90

1. The Trusteeship Council shall adopt its own rules of procedure, including the method of selecting its President.

2. The Trusteeship Council shall meet as required in accordance with its rules, which shall include provision for the convening of meetings on the request of a majority of its members.

Article 91

The Trusteeship Council shall, when appropriate, avail itself of the assistance of the Economic and Social Council and of the specialized agencies in regard to matters with which they are respectively concerned.

Chapter XIV
THE INTERNATIONAL COURT OF JUSTICE

Article 92

The International Court of Justice shall be the principal judicial organ of the

United Nations. It shall function in accordance with the annexed Statute, which is based upon the Statute of the Permanent Court of International Justice and forms an integral part of the present Charter.

Article 93

1. All Members of the United Nations are *ipso facto* parties to the Statute of the International Court of Justice.

2. A state which is not a Member of the United Nations may become a party to the Statue of the International Court of Justice on conditions to be determined in each case by the General Assembly upon the recommendation of the Security Council.

Article 94

1. Each Member of the United Nations undertakes to comply with the decision of the International Court of Justice in any case to which it is a party.

2. If any party to a case fails to perform the obligations incumbent upon it under a judgment rendered by the Court, the other party may have recourse to the Security Council, which may, if it deems necessary, make recommendations or decide upon measures to be taken to give effect to the judgment.

Article 95

Nothing in the present Charter shall prevent Members of the United Nations from entrusting the solution of their differences to other tribunals by virtue of agreements already in existence or which may be concluded in the future.

Article 96

1. The General Assembly or the Security Council may request the International Court of Justice to give an advisory opinion on any legal question.

2. Other organs of the United Nations and specialized agencies, which may at any time be so authorized by the General Assembly,

may also request advisory opinions of the Court on legal questions arising within the scope of their activities.

Chapter XV
THE SECRETARIAT

Article 97

The Secretariat shall comprise a Secretary-General and such staff as the Organization may require. The Secretary-General shall be appointed by the General Assembly upon the recommendation of the Security Council. He shall be the chief administrative officer of the Organization.

Article 98

The Secretary-General shall act in that capacity in all meetings of the General Assembly, of the Security Council, of the Economic and Social Council, and of the Trusteeship Council, and shall perform such other functions as are entrusted to him by these organs. The Secretary-General shall make an annual report to the General Assembly on the work of the Organization.

Article 99

The Secretary-General may bring to the attention of the Security Council any matter which in his opinion may threaten the maintenance of international peace and security.

Article 100

1. In the performance of their duties the Secretary-General and the staff shall not seek or receive instructions from any government or from any other authority external to the Organization. They shall refrain from any action which might reflect on their position as international officials responsible only to the Organization.

2. Each Member of the United Nations undertakes to respect the exclusively international character of the responsibilities of the Secretary-General and the staff and not to seek to influence them in the discharge of their responsibilities.

Article 101

1. The staff shall be appointed by the Secretary-General under regulations established by the General Assembly.

2. Appropriate staffs shall be permanently assigned to the Economic and Social Council, the Trusteeship Council, and as required, to other organs of the United Nations. These staffs shall form a part of the Secretariat.

3. The paramount consideration in the employment of the staff and in the determination of the conditions of service shall be the necessity of securing the highest standards of efficiency, competence, and integrity. Due regard shall be paid to the importance of recruiting the staff on as wide a geographical basis as possible.

Chapter XVI
MISCELLANEOUS PROVISIONS

Article 102

1. Every treaty and every international agreement entered into by any Member of the United Nations after the present Charter comes into force shall as soon as possible be registered with the Secretariat and published by it.

2. No party to any such treaty or international agreement which has not been registered in accordance with the provisions of paragraph 1 of this Article may invoke that treaty or agreement before any organ of the United Nations.

Article 103

In the event of a conflict between the obligations of the Members of the United Nations under the present Charter and their obligations under any other international agreement, their obligations under the present Charter shall prevail.

Article 104

The Organization shall enjoy in the territory of each of its Members such legal capacity as may be necessary for the exercise of its functions and the fulfillment of its purposes.

Article 105

1. The Organization shall enjoy in the territory of each of its Members such privileges and immunities as are necessary for the fulfillment of its purposes.

2. Representatives of the Members of the United Nations and officials of the Organization shall similarly enjoy such privileges and immunities as are necessary for the independent exercise of their functions in connection with the Organization.

3. The General Assembly may make recommendations with a view to determining the details of the application of paragraphs 1 and 2 of this Article or may propose conventions to the Members of the United Nations for this purpose.

Chapter XVII
TRANSITIONAL SECURITY ARRANGEMENTS

Article 106

Pending the coming into force of such special agreements referred to in Article 43 as in the opinion of the Security Council enable it to begin the exercise of its responsibilities under Article 42, the parties to the Four-Nation Declaration, signed at Moscow, October 30, 1943, and France, shall in accordance with the provisions of paragraph 5 of that Declaration, consult with one another and as occasion requires with other Members of the United Nations with a view to such joint action on behalf of the Organization as may be necessary for the purpose of maintaining international peace and security.

Article 107

Nothing in the present Charter shall invalidate or preclude action, in relation to any state which during the Second World War has been an enemy of any signatory to the present Charter, taken or authorized as a result of that war by the Governments having responsibility for such action.

Chapter XVIII
AMENDMENTS

Article 108

Amendments to the present Charter shall come into force for all Members of the United Nations when they have been adopted by a vote of two-thirds of the members of the General Assembly and ratified in accordance with their respective constitutional processes by two-thirds of the Members of the United Nations, including all the permanent members of the Security Council.

Article 109

1. A General Conference of the Members of the United Nations for the purpose of reviewing the present Charter may be held at a date and place to be fixed by a two-thirds vote of the members of the General Assembly and by a vote of any nine members of the Security Council. Each Member of the United Nations shall have one vote in the conference.

2. Any alteration of the present Charter recommended by a two-thirds vote of the conference shall take effect when ratified in accordance with their respective constitutional processes by two-thirds of the Members of the United Nations including all the permanent members of the Security Council.

3. If such a conference has not been held before the tenth annual session of the General Assembly following the coming into force of the present Charter, the proposal to call such a conference shall be placed on the agenda of that session of the General Assembly, and the conference shall be held if so decided by a majority vote of the members of the General Assembly and by a vote of any nine members of the Security Council.

Chapter XIX
RATIFICATION AND SIGNATURE

Article 110

1. The present Charter shall be ratified by the signatory states in accordance with their respective constitutional processes.

2. The ratifications shall be deposited with the Government of the United States of America, which shall notify all the signatory states of each deposit as well as the Secretary-General of the Organization when he has been appointed.

3. The present Charter shall come into force upon the deposit of ratifications by the Republic of China, France, The Union of Soviet Socialist Republics, the United Kingdom of Great Britain and Northern Ireland, and the United States of America, and by a majority of the other signatory states. A protocol of the ratifications deposited shall thereupon be drawn up by the Government of the United States of America which shall communicate copies thereof to all the signatory states.

4. The states signatory to the present Charter which ratify it after it has come into force will become original Members of the United Nations on the date of the deposit of their respective ratifications.

Article 111

The present Charter, of which the Chinese, French, Russian, English, and Spanish texts are equally authentic, shall remain deposited in the archives of the Government of the United States of America. Duly certified copies thereof shall be transmitted by that Government to the Governments of the other signatory states.

IN FAITH WHEREOF the representatives of the Governments of the United Nations have signed the present Charter.

DONE at the city of San Francisco the twenty-sixth day of June, one thousand nine hundred and forty-five.

STATUTE OF THE INTERNATIONAL COURT OF JUSTICE

Article 1

The International Court of Justice established by the Charter of the United Nations as the principal judicial organ of the United Nations shall be constituted and shall function in accordance with the provisions of the present Statute.

Chapter I
ORGANIZATION OF THE COURT

Article 2

The court shall be composed of a body of independent judges, elected regardless of their nationality from among persons of high moral character, who possess the qualifications required in their respective countries for appointment to the highest judicial offices, or are juris-consults of recognized competence in international law.

Article 3

1. The Court shall consist of fifteen members, no two of whom may be nationals of the same state.

2. A person who for the purposes of membership in the Court could be regarded as a national of more than one state shall be deemed to be a national of the one in which he ordinarily exercises civil and political rights.

Article 4

1. The members of the Court shall be elected by the General Assembly and by the Security Council from a list of persons nominated by the national groups in the Permanent Court of Arbitration, in accordance with the following provisions.

2. In the case of Members of the United Nations not represented in the Permanent Court of Arbitration, candidates shall be

nominated by national groups appointed for this purpose by their governments under the same conditions as those prescribed for members of the Permanent Court of Arbitration by Article 44 of the Convention of the Hague of 1907 for the pacific settlement of international disputes.

3. The conditions under which a state which is a party to the present Statute but is not a Member of the United Nations may participate in electing the members of the Court shall, in the absence of a special agreement, be laid down by the General Assembly upon recommendation of the Security Council.

Article 5

1. At least three months before the date of the election, the Secretary-General of the United Nations shall address a written request to the members of the Permanent Court of Arbitration belonging to the states which are parties to the present Statute, and to the members of the national groups appointed under Article 4, paragraph 2, inviting them to undertake, within a given time, by national groups, the nomination of persons in a position to accept the duties of a member of the Court.

2. No group may nominate more than four persons, not more than two of whom shall be of their own nationality. In no case may the number of candidates nominated by a group be more than double the number of seats to be filled.

Article 6

Before making these nominations, each national group is recommended to consult its highest court of justice, its legal faculties and schools of law, and its national academies and national sections of international academies devoted to the study of law.

Article 7

1. The Secretary-General shall prepare a list in alphabetical order of all the persons thus nominated. Save as provided in Article 12, paragraph 2, these shall be the only persons eligible.

2. The Secretary-General shall submit this list to the General Assembly and to the Security Council.

Article 8

The General Assembly and the Security Council shall proceed independently of one another to elect the members of the Court.

Article 9

At every election, the electors shall bear in mind not only that the persons to be elected should individually possess the qualifications required, but also that in the body as a whole the representation of the main forms of civilization and of the principal legal systems of the world should be assured.

Article 10

1. Those candidates who obtain an absolute majority of votes in the General Assembly and in the Security Council shall be considered as elected.

2. Any vote of the Security Council, whether for the election of judges or for the appointment of members of the conference envisaged in Article 12, shall be taken without any distinction between permanent and non-permanent members of the Security Council.

3. In the event of more than one national of the same state obtaining an absolute majority of the votes both of the General Assembly and of the Security Council, the eldest of these only shall be considered as elected.

Article 11

If, after the first meeting held for the purpose of the election, one or more seats remain to be filled, a second and, if necessary, a third meeting shall take place.

Article 12

1. If, after the third meeting, one or more seats still remain unfilled, a joint conference consisting of six members, three appointed by the General Assembly and three by the Security Council, may be formed at any time at the request of either the General Assembly or the Security Council, for the purpose of choosing by the vote of an absolute majority one name for each seat still vacant, to submit to the General Assembly and the Security Council for their respective acceptance.

2. If the joint conference is unanimously agreed upon any person who fulfills the required conditions, he may be included in its list, even though he was not included in the list of nominations referred to in Article 7.

3. If the joint conference is satisfied that it will not be successful in procuring an election, those members of the Court who have already been elected shall, within a period to be fixed by the Security Council, proceed to fill the vacant seats by selection from among those candidates who have obtained votes either in the General Assembly or in the Security Council.

4. In the event of an equality of votes among the judges, the eldest judge shall have a casting vote.

Article 13

1. The members of the Court shall be elected for nine years and may be re-elected; provided, however, that of the judges elected at the first election, the terms of five judges shall expire at the end of three years and the terms of five more judges shall expire at the end of six years.

2. The judges whose terms are to expire at the end of the above-mentioned initial periods of three and six years shall be chosen by lot to be drawn by the Secretary-General immediately after the first election has been completed.

3. The members of the Court shall continue to discharge their duties until their places have been filled. Though replaced, they shall finish any cases which they may have begun.

4. In the case of the resignation of a member of the Court, the resignation shall be addressed to the President of the Court for transmission to the Secretary-General. This last notification makes the place vacant.

Article 14

Vacancies shall be filled by the same method as that laid down for the first election subject to the following provision: the Secretary-General shall, within one month of the occurrence of the vacancy, proceed to issue the invitations provided for in Article 5, and the date of the election shall be fixed by the Security Council.

Article 15

A member of the Court elected to replace a member whose term of office has not expired shall hold office for the remainder of his predecessor's term.

Article 16

1. No member of the Court may exercise any political or administrative function, or engage in any other occupation of a professional nature.

2. Any doubt on this point shall be settled by the decision of the Court.

Article 17

1. No member of the Court may act as agent, counsel, or advocate in any case.

2. No member may participate in the decision of any case in which he has previously taken part as agent, counsel, or advocate for one of the parties, or as a member of a national or international court, or of a commission of enquiry, or in any other capacity.

3. Any doubt on this point shall be settled by the decision of the Court.

Article 18

1. No member of the Court can be dismissed unless, in the unanimous opinion of the other members, he has ceased to fulfill the required conditions.

2. Formal notification thereof shall be made to the Secretary-General by the Registrar.

3. This notification makes the place vacant.

Article 19

The members of the Court, when engaged on the business of the Court, shall enjoy diplomatic privileges and immunities.

Article 20

Every member of the Court shall, before taking up his duties, make a solemn declaration in open court that he will exercise his powers impartially and conscientiously.

Article 21

1. The Court shall elect its President and Vice-President for three years; they may be re-elected.

2. The Court shall appoint it Registrar and may provide for the appointment of such other officers as may be necessary.

Article 22

1. The seat of the Court shall be established at The Hague. This, however, shall not prevent the Court from sitting and exercising its functions elsewhere whenever the Court considers it desirable.

2. The President and the Registrar shall reside at the seat of the Court.

Article 23

1. The Court shall remain permanently in session, except during the judicial vacations, the dates and duration of which shall be fixed by the Court.

2. Members of the Court are entitled to periodic leave, the dates and duration of which shall be fixed by the Court, having in mind the distance between The Hague and the home of each judge.

3. Members of the Court shall be bound, unless they are on leave or prevented from attending by illness or other serious reasons duly explained to the President, to hold themselves permanently at the disposal of the Court.

Article 24

1. If, for some special reason, a member of the Court considers that he should not take part in the decision of a particular case, he shall so inform the President.

2. If the President considers that for some special reason one of the members of the Court should not sit in a particular case, he shall give him notice accordingly.

3. If in any such case the member of the Court and the President disagree, the matter shall be settled by the decision of the Court.

Article 25

1. The full Court shall sit except when it is expressly provided otherwise in the present Statute.

2. Subject to the condition that the number of judges available to constitute the Court is not thereby reduced below eleven, the Rules of the Court may provide for allowing one or more judges, according to circumstances and in rotation, to be dispensed from sitting.

3. A quorum of nine judges shall suffice to constitute the Court.

Article 26

1. The court may from time to time form one or more chambers, composed of three or more judges as the Court may determine, for dealing with particular categories of cases; for example, labor cases and cases relating to transit and communications.

2. The Court may at any time form a chamber for dealing with a particular case. The number of judges to constitute such a chamber shall be determined by the Court with the approval of the parties.

3. Cases shall be heard and determined by the chambers provided for in this Article if the parties so request.

Article 27

A judgment given by any of the chambers provided for in Articles 26 and 29 shall be considered as rendered by the Court.

Article 28

The chambers provided for in Articles 26 and 29 may, with the consent of the parties, sit and exercise their functions elsewhere than at The Hague.

Article 29

With a view to the speedy dispatch of business, the Court shall form annually a chamber composed of five judges which, at the request of the parties, may hear and determine cases by summary procedure. In addition, two judges shall be selected for the purpose of replacing judges who find it impossible to sit.

Article 30

1. The Court shall frame rules for carrying out its functions. In particular, it shall lay down rules of procedure.

2. The Rules of the Court may provide for assessors to sit with the Court or with any of its chambers, without the right to vote.

Article 31

1. Judges of the nationality of each of the parties shall retain their right to sit in the case before the Court.

2. If the Court includes upon the Bench a judge of the nationality of one of the parties, any other party may choose a person to sit as judge. Such person shall be chosen preferably from among those persons who have been nominated as candidates as provided in Articles 4 and 5.

3. If the Court includes upon the Bench no judge of the nationality of the parties, each of these parties may proceed to choose a judge as provided in paragraph 2 of this Article.

4. The provisions of this Article shall apply to the case of Articles 26 and 29. In such cases, the President shall request one or if necessary, two of the members of the Court forming the chamber to give place to the members of the Court of the nationality of the parties concerned, and failing such, or if they are unable to be present, to the judges specially chosen by the parties.

5. Should there be several parties in the same interest, they shall, for the purpose of the preceding provisions, be reckoned as one party only. Any doubt upon this point shall be settled by the decision of the Court.

6. Judges chosen as laid down in paragraphs 2, 3, and 4 of this Article shall fulfill the conditions required by Articles 2, 17 (paragraph 2), 20, and 24 of the present Statute. They shall take part in the decision on terms of complete equality with their colleagues.

Article 32

1. Each member of the Court shall receive an annual salary.

2. The President shall receive a special annual allowance.

3. The Vice-President shall receive a special allowance for every day on which he acts as President.

4. The judges chosen under Article 31, other than members of the Court, shall receive compensation for each day on which they exercise their functions.

5. These salaries, allowances, and compensation shall be fixed by the General Assembly. They may not be decreased during the term of office.

6. The salary of the Registrar shall be fixed by the General Assembly on the proposal of the Court.

7. Regulations made by the General Assembly shall fix the conditions under which retirement pensions may be given to members of the Court and to the Registrar, and the conditions under which members of the Court and the Registrar shall have their travelling expenses refunded.

8. The above salaries, allowances, and compensation shall be free of all taxation.

Article 33

The expenses of the Court shall be borne by the United Nations in such a manner as shall be decided by the General Assembly.

Chapter II
COMPETENCE OF THE COURT

Article 34

1. Only states may be parties in cases before the Court.

2. The Court, subject to and in conformity with its Rules, may request of public international organizations information relevant to cases before it, and shall receive such information presented by such organizations on their own initiative.

3. Whenever the construction of the constituent instrument of a public international organization or of an international convention adopted thereunder is in question in a case before the Court, the Registrar shall so notify the public international organization concerned and shall communicate to it copies of all the written proceedings.

Article 35

1. The Court shall be open to the states parties to the present Statute.

2. The conditions under which the court shall be open to other states shall, subject to the special provisions contained in treaties in force, be laid down by the Security Council, but in no case shall such conditions place the parties in a position of inequality before the Court.

3. When a state which is not a Member of the United Nations is a party to a case, the Court shall fix the amount which that party is to contribute towards the expenses of the Court. This provision shall not apply if such state is bearing a share of the expenses of the Court.

Article 36

1. The jurisdiction of the Court comprises all cases which the parties refer to it and all matters specially provided for in the Charter of the United Nations or in treaties and conventions in force.

2. The states parties to the present Statute may at any time declare that they recognize as compulsory *ipso facto* and without special agreement, in relation to any other state accepting the same obligation, the jurisdiction of the Court in all legal disputes concerning.:

a. the interpretation of a treaty;

b. any question of international law;

c.   the existence of any fact which, if established, would constitute a breach of an international obligation;

d.   the nature or extent of the reparation to be made for the breach of an international obligation.

3.   The declarations referred to above may be made unconditionally or on condition of reciprocity on the part of several or certain states, or for a certain time.

4.   Such declarations shall be deposited with the Secretary-General of the United Nations, who shall transmit copies thereof to the parties to the Statute and to the Registrar of the Court.

5.   Declarations made under Article 36 of the Statute of the Permanent Court of International Justice and which are still in force shall be deemed, as between the parties to the present Statute, to be acceptances of the compulsory jurisdiction of the International Court of Justice for the period which they still have to run and in accordance with their terms.

6.   In the event of a dispute as to whether the Court has jurisdiction, the matter shall be settled by the decision of the Court.

Article 37

Whenever a treaty or convention in force provides for reference of a matter to a tribunal to have been instituted by the League of Nations, or to the Permanent Court of International Justice, the matter shall, as between the parties to the present Statute, be referred to the International Court of Justice.

Article 38

1.   The Court, whose function is to decide in accordance with international law such disputes as are submitted to it, shall apply:

a.   international conventions, whether general or particular, establishing rules expressly recognized by the contesting states;

b.   international custom, as evidence of a general practice accepted as law;

c. the general principles of law recognized by civilized nations;

d. subject to the provisions of Article 59, judicial decisions and the teachings of the most highly qualified publicists of the various nations, as subsidiary means for the determination of rules of law.

2. This provision shall not prejudice the power of the Court to decide a case *ex aequo et bono*, if the parties agree thereto.

Chapter III
PROCEDURE

Article 39

1. The official languages of the Court shall be French and English. If the parties agree that the case shall be conducted in French, the judgment shall be delivered in French. If the parties agree that the case shall be conducted in English, the judgment shall be delivered in English.

2. In the absence of an agreement as to which language shall be employed, each party may, in the pleadings, use the language which it prefers; the decision of the Court shall be given in French and English. In this case the Court shall at the same time determine which of the two texts shall be considered as authoritative.

3. The Court shall, at the request of any party, authorize a language other than French or English to be used by that party.

Article 40

1. Cases are brought before the court, as the case may be, either by notification of the special agreement or by a written application addressed to the Registrar. In either case the subject of the dispute and the parties shall be indicated.

2. The Registrar shall forthwith communicate the application to all concerned.

3. He shall also notify the Members of the United Nations through the Secretary-General, and also any other states entitled to appear before the Court.

Article 41

1. The Court shall have the power to indicate, if it considers that circumstances so require, any provisional measures which ought to be taken to preserve the respective rights of either party.

2. Pending the final decision, notice of the measures suggested shall forthwith be given to the parties and to the Security Council.

Article 42

1. The parties shall be represented by agents.

2. They may have the assistance of counsel or advocates before the Court.

3. The agents, counsel, and advocates of parties before the Court shall enjoy the privileges and immunities necessary to the independent exercise of their duties.

Article 43

1. The procedure shall consist of two parts: written and oral.

2. The written proceedings shall consist of the communication to the Court and to the parties of memorials, counter-memorials and, if necessary, replies; also all papers and documents in support.

3. These communications shall be made through the Registrar, in the order and within the time fixed by the Court.

4. A certified copy of every document produced by one party shall be communicated to the other party.

5. The oral proceedings shall consist of the hearing by the Court of witnesses, experts, agents, counsel, and advocates.

Article 44

1. For the service of all notices upon persons other than the agents, counsel, and advocates, the Court shall apply direct to the government of the state upon whose territory the notice has to be served.

2. The same provision shall apply whenever steps are to be taken to procure evidence on the spot.

Article 45

The hearing shall be under the control of the President or, if he is unable to preside, of the Vice-President; if neither is able to preside, the senior judge present shall preside.

Article 46

The hearing in Court shall be public, unless the court shall decide otherwise, or unless the parties demand that the public be not admitted.

Article 47

1. Minutes shall be made at each hearing and signed by the Registrar and the President.

2. These minutes alone shall be authentic.

Article 48

The Court shall make orders for the conduct of the case, shall decide the form and time in which each party must conclude its arguments, and make all arrangements connected with the taking of evidence.

Article 49

The Court may, even before the hearing begins, call upon the agents to produce any document or to supply any explanations. Formal note shall be taken of any refusal.

Article 50

The Court may, at any time, entrust any individual, body, bureau, commission, or other organization that it may select, with the task of carrying out an enquiry or giving an expert opinion.

Article 51

During the hearing any relevant questions are to be put to the witnesses and experts under the conditions laid down by the Court in the rules of procedure referred to in Article 30.

Article 52

After the Court has received the proofs and evidence within the time specified for the purpose, it may refuse to accept any further oral or written evidence that one party may desire to present unless the other side consents.

Article 53

1. Whenever one of the parties does not appear before the Court, or fails to defend its case, the other party may call upon the Court to decide in favor of its claim.

2. The Court must, before doing so, satisfy itself, not only that it has jurisdiction in accordance with Articles 36 and 27, but also that the claim is well founded in fact and law.

Article 54

1. When, subject to the control of the Court, the agents, counsel, and advocates have completed their presentation of the case, the President shall declare the hearing closed.

2. The Court shall withdraw to consider the judgment.

3. The deliberations of the Court shall take place in private and remain secret.

Article 55

1. All questions shall be decided by a majority of the judges present.

2. In the event of an equality of votes, the President or the judge who acts in his place shall have a casting vote.

Article 56

1. The judgment shall state the reasons on which it is based.

2. It shall contain the names of the judges who have taken part in the decision.

Article 57

If the judgment does not represent in whole or in part the unanimous opinion of the judges, any judge shall be entitled to deliver a separate opinion.

Article 58

The judgment shall be signed by the President and by the Registrar. It shall be read in open court, due notice having been given to the agents.

Article 59

The decision of the Court has no binding force except between the parties and in respect of that particular case.

Article 60

The judgment is final and without appeal. In the event of dispute as to the meaning or scope of the judgment, the Court shall construe it upon the request of any party.

Article 61

An application for revision of a judgment may be made only when it is based upon the discovery of some fact of such a nature as to be a decisive factor, which fact was, when the judgment was given, unknown to the Court and also to the party claiming revision, always provided that such ignorance was not due to negligence.

3. The proceedings for revision shall be opened by a judgment of the Court expressly recording the existence of the new fact, recognizing that it has such a character as to lay the case open to revision, and declaring the application admissible on this ground.

4. The Court may require previous compliance with the terms of the judgment before it admits proceedings in revision.

5. The application for revision must be made at latest within six months of the discovery of the new fact.

6. No application for revision may be made after the lapse of ten years from the date of the judgment.

Article 62

1. Should a state consider that it has an interest of a legal nature which may be affected by the decision in the case, it may submit a request to the Court to be permitted to intervene.

2. It shall be for the Court to decide upon this request.

Article 63

1. Whenever the construction of a convention to which states other than those concerned in the case are parties is in question, the Registrar shall notify all such states forthwith.

2. Every state so notified has the right to intervene in the proceedings; but if it uses this right, the construction given by the judgment will be equally binding upon it.

Article 64

Unless otherwise decided by the Court, each party shall bear its own costs.

Chapter IV
ADVISORY OPINIONS

Article 65

1. The Court may give an advisory opinion on any legal question at the request of whatever body may be authorized by or in accordance with the Charter of the United Nations to make such a request.

2. Questions upon which the advisory opinion of the Court is asked shall be laid before the Court by means of a written request containing an exact statement of the question upon which an opinion is required, and accompanied by all documents likely to throw light upon the question.

Article 66

1. The Registrar shall forthwith give notice of the request for an advisory opinion to all states entitled to appear before the Court.

2. The Registrar shall also, by means of a special and direct communication, notify any state entitled to appear before the Court or international organization considered by the Court, or, should it not be sitting, by the President, as likely to be able to furnish information on the question that the Court will be prepared to receive, within a time limit to be fixed by the President, written statements or to hear, at a public sitting to be held for the purpose, oral statements relating to the question.

3. Should any such state entitled to appear before the Court have failed to receive the special communication referred to in paragraph 2 of this Article, such state may express a desire to submit a written statement or to be heard; and the Court will decide.

4. States and organizations having presented written or oral statements or both shall be permitted to comment on the statements made by other states or organizations in the form, to

the extent, and within the time limits which the Court, or, should it not be sitting, the President, shall decide in each particular case. Accordingly, the Registrar shall in due time communicate any such written statements to states and organizations having submitted similar statements.

Article 67

The Court shall deliver its advisory opinions in open court, notice having been given to the Secretary-General and to the representatives of Members of the United Nations, of other states and of international organizations immediately concerned.

Article 68

In the exercise of its advisory functions the Court shall further be guided by the provisions of the present Statute which apply in contentious cases to the extent to which it recognizes them to be applicable.

Chapter V
AMENDMENT

Article 69

Amendments to the present Statute shall be effected by the same procedure as is provided by the Charter of the United Nations for amendments to that Charter, subject however to any provisions which the General Assembly upon recommendation of the Security Council may adopt concerning the participation of states which are parties to the present Statute but are not Members of the United Nations.

Article 70

The Court shall have power to propose such amendments of the present Statute as it may deem necessary through written communications to the Secretary-General for consideration in conformity with the provisions of Article 69.

About the Author

Joseph A. Bagnall has served as an educator, teaching United States History and American Government at the college level for many years. His past publications include:

- *Depression Dialogue: An Anthology of Representative Political Dialogue of the Depression Decade,* William C. Brown, 1965.

- (co-author) *United States History: The Relevant Issues,* William C. Brown, 1973;

- *President John F. Kennedy's Grand and Global Alliance: World Order for the New Century,* University Press of America, 1992.

- *The Politics of Survival: Resolving the Seven Deadly Trends,* McGraw-Hill, 1997.

- *The Kennedy Option: Pursuit of World Law,* University Press of America, 2002.

He has also written and produced a television documentary titled *John F. Kennedy's Lost Pathway to Peace,* which aired on KCET Los Angeles and on a number of other PBS stations. It also aired on TBS on the 69th and 70th anniversaries of JFK's birth.

Dr. Bagnall was interviewed by Charles Osgood, on the CBS Radio Network, on the 75th anniversary of President Kennedy's birth.